Persevere and Prevail Like
Mukesh Ambani

Rajiv Agarwal is a family business consultant with more than twenty years of experience. Considered a leading expert on family business in India, he has advised more than 1,500 families on succession, strategy and continuity. Currently a professor of Family Business, Strategy and Entrepreneurship at SP Jain Institute of Management & Research (SPJIMR), Mumbai, which is also his alma mater, Agarwal got his PhD from BITS Pilani and is an alumnus of Harvard Business School. He has been the visiting professor at IIM Kozhikode and IIM Indore, and an expert advisor on the Board of Academics, Department of Management, Nirma University, Ahmedabad. He also writes in various publications on topics related to family business.

Also by the same author

Think, Lead & Strategize Like Kumar Mangalam Birla
Lead with Purpose Like Anand Mahindra
Succeed to Inspire Like the Tatas
Believe to Succeed Like Azim Premji

Persevere and Prevail Like
Mukesh Ambani

Rajiv Agarwal

Published by
Rupa Publications India Pvt. Ltd 2020
7/16, Ansari Road, Daryaganj
New Delhi 110002

Sales centres:
Allahabad Bengaluru Chennai
Hyderabad Jaipur Kathmandu
Kolkata Mumbai

Copyright © Rajiv Agarwal 2020

The views and opinions expressed in this book are the author's own
and the facts are as reported by him which have been
verified to the extent possible, and the publishers are not in
any way liable for the same.

All rights reserved.

No part of this publication may be reproduced, transmitted,
or stored in a retrieval system, in any form or by any means,
electronic, mechanical, photocopying, recording or otherwise,
without the prior permission of the publisher.

ISBN: 978-93-5333-825-1

First impression 2020

10 9 8 7 6 5 4 3 2 1

The moral right of the author has been asserted.

Printed at Parksons Graphics Pvt. Ltd, Mumbai

This book is sold subject to the condition that it shall not,
by way of trade or otherwise, be lent, resold, hired out, or otherwise
circulated, without the publisher's prior consent, in any form of
binding or cover other than that in which it is published.

CONTENTS

Preface *vii*
Introduction *ix*

1. The Person: Mukesh Ambani 1
2. Mukesh Ambani's Management Style 20
3. What Are the Biggest Learnings for Mukesh Ambani? 43
4. Time as a Competitive Advantage: Learn the Value of Time 49
5. Flexibility and Integration of the Value Chain 54
6. Look to the Future for New Opportunities: Change the Strategy to Future-Proof the Company 64
7. The Power of Teams 79

8.	Reduce Debt: Be Responsive to the Environment	86
9.	Build World-scale Capacities	92
10.	Think Big, Dream Big	98
11.	Focus on World-class Capacities, Lowest Costs: The Jamnagar Complex	102
12.	Diversification Into Retail: Focus on Buying Iconic Brands to Consolidate Retail Push	115
13.	Eye on the Future: Always Hunting for Value Addition	121
14.	Change Business Model to Be Relevant: Oil-to-chemicals (O2C) Strategy	131
15.	Creating Opportunities: The Green Belt at Jamnagar	143
16.	The Next Generation: Involve Them Young	147
17.	Values	159
18.	A Low-cost Model for Indian Markets: If It Does Not Exist, Build One!	164

Summary 168

PREFACE

This was not an easy book to write, especially when all the material sought for this book was only from published sources. While Mukesh Ambani, the Indian industrialist, and supposedly the country's richest, is media-shy, his companies and moves are actively reported in the press, almost daily! There are multiple articles in the media along with stories about his life. These anecdotes are many, but they also bring with them the responsibility for their authenticity. These could be dubious even if reported in the media. Readers are advised to note that all the instances mentioned in this book are taken from published sources in the media, and one needs to exercise discretion accordingly, especially concerning the authenticity of their facts. While every care has been taken to cite the sources, their authenticity is to be regarded with these limitations in mind.

Additionally, readers would appreciate that the earlier contributions of the late Dhirubhai Ambani have been mentioned extensively. For the instances relating to the period before the split between the two brothers, Mukesh and Anil, individual contributions are difficult to ascertain and give credit to, and that is a limitation in this book. However, these limitations should not be a constraint in the pursuit of lessons one can learn from Mukesh Ambani.

INTRODUCTION

Mukesh Ambani has been acknowledged as the richest man in India. His story is unprecedented and his vision and achievements redefine the term 'large-scale'. He has attempted to dream big, matched second only by his father (Dhirubhai Ambani's) vision of growing his company—Reliance. And he has achieved a magnitude of success, which perhaps not even his father would have envisaged. Or maybe he had? No one knows for sure, but what is definite is that by the time the world understands the genius behind whatever decision Mukesh executes he has already moved far ahead!

His success is amazing and admired by both friend and foe. His new ventures only seem to be even more audacious and may leave some shaking their heads in disbelief. But Mukesh has proven them wrong on multiple occasions.

In October 2005, the Reliance group was split between the Ambani brothers, and elder brother Mukesh got Reliance Industries and Indian Petrochemicals Corporation Limited (IPCL). And that marked the beginning of his journey.[1]

With a net worth of around $54 billion, Mukesh became the first Indian, and the only Asian, to figure on the global top 10 of Hurun's Rich List in 2019. He was also ranked 13th on the Forbes billionaire list, in a long list of many such lists where his name appears prominently. He was included in *Time* magazine's 100 Most Influential People in April 2019, along with Facebook's Mark Zuckerberg, US President Donald Trump and Michelle Obama, the former US first lady.[2]

---

[1] Moneycontrol News, 'Podcast: Digging Deep, the business of family—the Ambanis', moneycontrol.com, 21 June 2019, accessed 10 August 2019, https://www.moneycontrol.com/news/business/companies/podcast-digging-deep-the-business-of-family-the-ambanis-2618621.html

[2] ET Online, 'Mukesh Ambani: Asia's richest man keeps his friends close, has a fixed salary since 10 years, and is a favourite headline name', *The Economic Times*, 19 April 2019, accessed 16 August 2019, https://economictimes.indiatimes.com/magazines/panache/mukesh-ambani-asias-richest-man-keeps-his-friends-close-has-a-fixed-salary-since-10-years-and-is-a-favourite-headline-name/articleshow/68939829.cms

Introduction

There are many stories surrounding Reliance and Mukesh. The intention in this book is for business owners and students of management to understand and learn from the achievements of this industrialist. The purpose is to have a book which facilitates learning, and not be just a journalistic piece on the industrialist. Hence, I have taken the liberty of including a few select achievements which I consider as offering the most learning. There could be other instances which may not have been included due to space constraints, which is the limitation of this book. I am sure that had I had an opportunity to interview Mr Ambani, some of the content would have been different. Since all the content in this book is from public published sources, this is also a limitation.

Like any successful industrialist, Mukesh has both admirers and detractors. Whichever side one may listen to, the fact remains that the spectacular success of Mukesh offers learning for every management student or a business owner. And we seek to explore and understand what his actions have been, as reported in various public sources of information. These are some of the things that can be learned from some of the decisions he made.

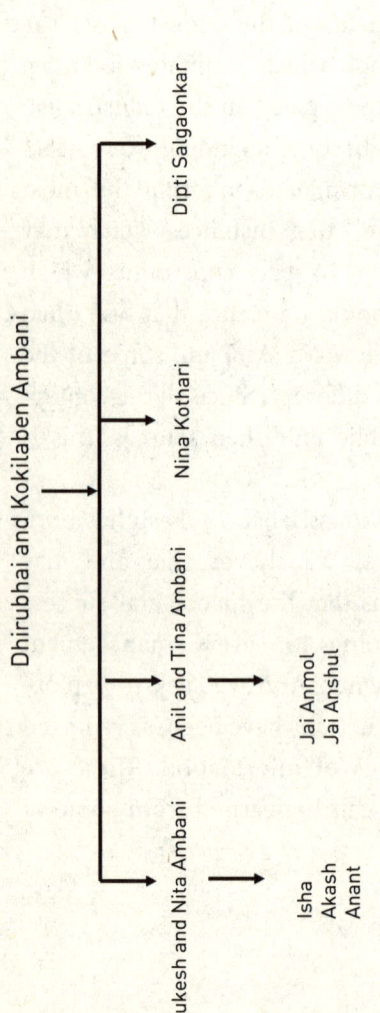

1
THE PERSON: MUKESH AMBANI[1]

Mukesh Ambani's current success may make it easy for most people to forget the hardships that the Ambani family has been through. The family experienced what may be called a rags-to-riches story, starting with the patriarch Dhirubhai, whose story still inspires every entrepreneur. Mukesh experienced it first-hand, as a child, before they moved to the

---

[1] 'Billionaire birthday boy Mukesh Ambani is not an MBA; pure vegetarian, teetotaller has salary frozen at Rs 15 cr pa since 2009!' Businesstoday.in, 19 April 2019, accessed 7 August 2019, https://www.businesstoday.in/current/corporate/reliance-industries-ril-chairman-mukesh-ambani-birthday/story/338674.html

Bhuleshwar neighbourhood in Mumbai (then known as Bombay) when he was seven. The progression of the Ambani family began when they moved from Bhuleshwar to the upmarket Usha Kiran at Altamount Road, then to Sea Wind in Cuffe Parade and from there, Mukesh and his family comprising wife Nita and their three children moved to their present home, Antilia, a 27-storey building, referred to by some as the most expensive real estate in the world.[2]

Mukesh is the eldest son of Dhirubhai and Kokilaben. He was born on 19 April 1957, in Aden, Yemen. His father, Dhirubhai Ambani, made his mark in the Indian industrial environment, becoming one of the fastest-growing industrialists, in the 1980s. Dirubhai set up companies with unheard-of capacities, targeting export markets. He did not receive any support from banks, so he went to the stock market to raise funds. He started ensuring that his investors got capital appreciation by the rising stock prices, besides

---

[2]ET Online, 'Mukesh Ambani: Asia's richest man keeps his friends close, has a fixed salary since 10 years, and is a favourite headline name', *The Economic Times*, 19 April 2019, accessed 16 August 2019, https://economictimes.indiatimes.com/magazines/panache/mukesh-ambani-asias-richest-man-keeps-his-friends-close-has-a-fixed-salary-since-10-years-and-is-a-favourite-headline-name/articleshow/68939829.cms

The Person: Mukesh Ambani

the regular dividends. This ensured a good response for all his stock-market offerings. This also made him the favourite amongst his investors. His Annual General Meetings (AGMs) were held in football stadiums to accommodate all the investors who attended it. Arising from very humble beginnings, (he often used to call himself a member of the Zero Club, since that's what he started with[3]), he came to Bombay from Aden, with Mukesh and Kokilaben.

Mukesh's mother, Kokilaben, now rules over the family household, takes the grandchildren on holidays and sits in the front rows of the AGMs. This is a far cry from the earlier days, of looking after the children, cooking and looking after the household, while Dhirubhai was looking after the business and travelling between Delhi and the various manufacturing plants.[4]

Mukesh did his bachelor's in Chemical Engineering from the Institute of Chemical Technology (ICT, formerly known as UDCT), Matunga, in 1979.[5] He was conferred with an honorary doctorate of science

---

[3]Gita Piramal, *Business Maharajas*, Penguin UK, 2000
[4]Ibid.
[5]'Mukesh Ambani gets doctorate from ICT', 19 February 2015, *UDCT Alumni Association*, accessed 29 October 2019, https://www.udctalumni.org.in/newsroom/news/Mukesh-Ambani-gets-doctorate-from-ICT-4.dz#

by the same institution in 2015. He then enrolled at Stanford University for an MBA in 1980. However, on his father's request, he cut short his MBA and returned to India to head the Patalganga project, in 1981.[6]

Mukesh married Nayantara Dalal, a schoolteacher, now better known as Nita, in 1985.[7] Nita would play a very important role, later on, heading some important initiatives in Reliance.

Their story, according to the media, states that Dhirubhai had seen Nita in a dance programme and had later called to ask if she would meet his son. Later on, during their courtship, Mukesh was at Patalganga building the plant. He would drive his green Fiat for three hours to meet his fiancée. He is said to have popped the question to Nita at a busy intersection in Mumbai.[8]

They have two sons, Anant and Akash, and a daughter, Isha. Isha is married to Anand Piramal, son

---

[6]ET Online, 'Mukesh Ambani: Asia's richest man keeps his friends close, has a fixed salary since 10 years, and is a favourite headline name', *The Economic Times*, 19 April 2019, accessed 16 August 2019, https://economictimes.indiatimes.com/magazines/panache/mukesh-ambani-asias-richest-man-keeps-his-friends-close-has-a-fixed-salary-since-10-years-and-is-a-favourite-headline-name/articleshow/68939829.cms
[7]Ibid.
[8]Ibid.

of the industrialist, Ajay Piramal. Akash is married to Shloka Mehta, daughter of diamantaire Russell Mehta, managing director of Rosy Blue Diamonds.[9]

Mukesh is a pure vegetarian and a teetotaller. His favourite eating place is Mysore Café in Matunga, which he has been frequenting since his college (UDCT) days. He is known to lead an unassuming lifestyle.

There is a newspaper report of an occasion in New York, when Mukesh and a Stanford classmate, Akhil Gupta were dining at Nobu (a very high-end renowned Japanese restaurant). Mukesh being vegetarian found the meal bland and was picking at the dishes. After the meal was over, Akhil recalls him saying, 'That was nice. Now should we go have dinner?' [10]

Mukesh prefers comfort food and has stated on an occasion, 'I still have to eat my dal, roti, chawal. I

---

[9]ET Now Digital, 'Meet Shloka Mehta: The GenNext Ambani bahu is worth USD 18 million', ETNOWNEWS.com, 26 March 2018, accessed 29 October 2019, https://www.timesnownews.com/business-economy/companies/article/meet-shloka-mehta-the-genext-ambani-bahu-is-worth-usd-18-million/211171

[10]Anand Giridharadas, 'Indian to the Core, and an Oligarch', *The New York Times*, New York edition, 15 June 2008, accessed 15 August 2019, https:// www.nytimes.com/2008/06/15/business/worldbusiness/15ambani.html

have just not developed those tastes'.[11]

He is also known not to carry a wallet or any cash, as he always has someone to pay for him.[12] This habit has been with him since he was growing up!

He is known to have interests which are rooted in India. He dresses in simple clothes and is not a fan of any brand. He is usually seen in a white shirt and black trousers, except during his AGMs or other formal functions, where he dons a suit with his lucky red-and-white chequered tie!

Nandan Nilekani, of Infosys, had stated in a newspaper article that he (Mukesh) was self-confident, and would not depend on Western symbols to prove his status in society or to impress anyone.[13]

He is known to be deeply religious and prays every day. Mukesh portrays this sense of being grounded with preferences and habits which are still very simple in his personal life.

His childhood was spent with his younger

---

[11]Ibid.

[12]FC Bureau, 'Somebody always pays for me: Mukesh Ambani', accessed September 2019, https://www.mydigitalfc.com/fc-weekend/somebody-always-pays-me-mukesh-ambani

[13]Anand Giridharadas, 'Indian to the Core, and an Oligarch', *The New York Times*, New York edition, 15 June 2008, accessed 15 August 2019, https://www.nytimes.com/2008/06/15/business/worldbusiness/15ambani.html

brother, Anil, in a two-bedroom apartment in the neighbourhood of Bhuleshwar, in Mumbai. His father was in the yarn trading business, which required one to be constantly alert for opportunities. The import of yarn required getting licences which were hard to come by and needed a good understanding of the bureaucracy.[14]

These early childhood experiences shaped him in a manner that he would not understand at the time. But these may have played a very significant role in developing what one could call the fire in the belly, namely, the instinct to fight and succeed, typically found amongst first-generation entrepreneurs, even though he enjoys all the privileges of a second-generation billionaire.[15]

His education was similarly influenced. His father was worried about his children growing up pampered. So, he hired a tutor, Mahendrabhai Vyas, a teacher from the New Era School for their all-round development.

His main responsibility was to spend three hours every day, taking Mukesh and Anil on class field trips in public transport, playing hockey, football and other sports, watching matches at Cooperage Ground and

---

[14]Ibid.
[15]Ibid.

exploring the city of Mumbai. There was also the annual 15-day visit to a village. Mukesh recalls this to be a very good learning experience, even though they never studied during these field trips.

Dhirubhai always believed in learning the ropes by experience and not in academic institutions. This could have been one reason for his calling Mukesh back to India, midway through his Stanford MBA, to take care of a yarn manufacturing project. According to a story, Mukesh had wanted to spend a year working in the US after he finished his education and asked Dhirubhai if he could join in around 18 months. To which Dhirubhai is said to have replied that the project could not wait and he was going ahead. Mukesh heard this and decided to join the family company leaving his education.

Even during this time, his dedication to his work drew praise. He was working in a village, sleeping in a trailer on-site and balanced his big dreams with attention to detail.[16] K.V. Kamath, then a banker to the Ambanis, observed Mukesh closely and found him to be a perpetual learner and an exceedingly good listener. Another person found him to be hands-on, someone who likes to get his hands dirty. He compared Mukesh

---

[16]Ibid.

The Person: Mukesh Ambani

to a shopkeeper who wanted to sit at the cash counter and see what was happening.

Ravi Venkatesan, the then chairman of Microsoft India, had said that Mukesh's forte was being able to see the bigger picture and also observe details at the grass-roots level. He also stated that he had not seen too many people with the ability to think in terms of very large scale and match it with an aptitude to take such high risks.[17] Mukesh earned recognition when he proved his ability and completed the Patalganga plant on schedule.

Mukesh stated that his father had made him a board member at around the age of 18. As he was involved with Reliance right from the time it was a textile company, Mukesh had always felt that he had built the company with his father, instead of thinking that he had just inherited it. He also had, to his advantage, the fact that his father had accepted him as a first-generation partner, instead of a second-generation family member. He got full freedom, including the freedom to take big risks. On these lines, Mukesh recalls being told, 'Here, take 80 crores rupees

---

[17] Anand Giridharadas, 'Indian to the Core, and an Oligarch', *The New York Times*, New York edition, 15 June 2008, accessed 15 August 2019, https://www.nytimes.com/2008/06/15/business/worldbusiness/15ambani.html

and build a polyester plant[18]. This was at a time when Mukesh had just entered the business and did not have any prior experience!

Over time, he has diversified the family business from the earlier businesses of petrochemicals, refining, and oil and gas to telecom and retail.[19]

Mukesh is known to be a diligent worker, reaching his office at noon, and working till midnight. But in spite of his busy schedule, he prefers to spend Sundays catching up with his family.[20]

He values this time with the family and has attributed this trait of his to the time spent with his father while growing up. Their Sundays used to be spent travelling out somewhere or communing with nature, a habit that has stayed with him till date. In fact, the family holidays were frequently at Kruger National Park in South Africa, known for its wildlife.

---

[18] Ibid.

[19] Businesstoday.in, 'Billionaire birthday boy Mukesh Ambani is not an MBA; pure vegetarian, teetotaller has salary frozen at Rs 15 cr pa since 2009!', 19 April 2019, accessed 7 August 2019, https://www.businesstoday.in/current/corporate/reliance-industries-ril-chairman-mukesh-ambani-birthday/story/338674.html

[20] '12 things you probably didn't know about Mukesh Ambani', msn.com, 2 July 2019, accessed 9 August 2019, https://www.msn.com/en-in/money/photos/12-things-you-probably-didnt-know-about-mukesh-ambani/ss-BBQvk4r#image=6

HIS RESIDENCE

Mukesh's current home is Antilia, a 27-storey building, rated by some as the most expensive real estate in the world.[21] The building is reportedly named after the mythical island in the Atlantic Ocean and is estimated to be amongst the world's most expensive building at almost $1 billion. It is supposed to require a staff of 600 to maintain its 400,000 square feet over its 27 storeys, a multistorey garage for 168 cars and three helipads. The lobby at the residence has nine elevators and contains terraced gardens, a spa, a temple, gymnasiums, a yoga studio and a 50-seater movie theatre.[22] (Mukesh is a movie buff and is known to watch three movies a week.)

---

[21]ET Online, 'Mukesh Ambani: Asia's richest man keeps his friends close, has a fixed salary since 10 years, and is a favourite headline name', *The Economic Times*, 19 April 2019, accessed 16 August 2019, https://economictimes.indiatimes.com/magazines/panache/mukesh-ambani-asias-richest-man-keeps-his-friends-close-has-a-fixed-salary-since-10-years-and-is-a-favourite-headline-name/articleshow/68939829.cms

[22]Rupande Mehta, 'What India's Super-Rich Can Learn From Their Western Counterparts', *The Blog, Huffpost* online, 10 July 2015, accessed 23 September 2019, https://www.huffingtonpost.in/rupande-mehta/indias-rich-famous-the-sh_b_7695720.html

MUKESH AMBANI ON MONEY

In a newspaper article,[23] while addressing the Hindustan Times Leadership Summit (HTLS), Mukesh stated that he did not consider money as important as resources. He further stated that he had since childhood, school life and even to the current day, not carried any cash or credit cards with him for any transactions. This was because he always had someone else paying for him. He also clarified that he did not like the labels or the titles that had been used while referring to him. For him, money used as a resource gave his company some flexibility and enabled his company to take risks. Of course, the article also stated that the audience found his statement hard to believe—these words which sounded amazingly humble, coming from someone who has been considered the richest man in India!

STAYING TRUE TO STRONG FAMILY VALUES

In March 2019, Mukesh intervened and paid a cheque of $67 million towards an outstanding debt on behalf

---

[23]FC Bureau, 'Somebody always pays for me: Mukesh Ambani', FC Weekend, *Financial Chronicle*, 2 December 2017, accessed 23 September 2019, https://www.mydigitalfc.com/fc-weekend/somebody-always-pays-me-mukesh-ambani

The Person: Mukesh Ambani

of his younger brother, Anil, a day before a court-imposed deadline. If this payment had not been made, Anil faced the possibility of spending three months behind bars. This money came from Mukesh in a personal capacity.[24] Anil expressed deep gratitude. 'My sincere and heartfelt thanks to my respected elder brother, Mukesh, and Nita, for standing by me during these trying times, and demonstrating the importance of staying true to our strong family values by extending this timely support... I and my family are grateful we have moved beyond the past, and are deeply touched with this gesture.'[25]

---

[24]Joanna Slater, 'Family ties: Asia's richest man helps pay $67 million to keep his brother out of jail', *The Washington Post*, 19 March 2019, accessed 23 September 2019, https://www.washingtonpost.com/world/asia_pacific/family-ties-indias-richest-man-helps-pay-67-million-to-keep-his-brother-out-of-jail/2019/03/19/e7e39e20-4a36-11e9-b871-978e5c757325_story.html?noredirect=on

[25]Devina Sengupta, 'Anil Ambani thanks elder brother Mukesh Ambani for paying Ericsson dues', *The Economic Times*, 19 March 2019, accessed 23 September 2019, https://economictimes.indiatimes.com/industry/telecom/telecom-news/anil-ambani-thanks-elder-brother-mukesh-ambani-for-paying-ericsson-dues/articleshow/68470050.cms

SETTING A PERSONAL EXAMPLE

In July 2019, it was reported that he had continued to cap his salary at ₹15 crore, a decision that he had taken in 2009. The annual report had stated that this was in line with his desire to continue to set a personal example for moderation in managerial compensation levels.[26]

HUMILITY

Mukesh had once stated in a video interview, that he had felt that the new generation is changing, and his children had told him, 'Dad, you don't get it.'[27] He admitted that he would have never had the courage to tell his father these words. This also shows his open-mindedness, humility and desire to learn, in a new environment. He is also known to be a voracious reader.

---

[26] Amritha Pillay, 'RIL has built foundation for next decade in FY19, says Mukesh Ambani', *Business Standard*, 21 July 2019, accessed 29 July 2019, https://www.business-standard.com/article/companies/ril-has-built-foundation-for-next-decade-in-fy19-says-mukesh-ambani-119072100035_1.html.

[27] SIFY, 'Money never meant much to me, says Mukesh Ambani', *Sify Finance*, 3 December 2017, accessed 23 September 2019, https://www.sify.com/finance/money-never-meant-much-to-me-says-mukesh-ambani-news-finance-rmboueddeadgj.html

(In a TV interview, he stated that he was currently reading about blockchain technology.)

LEARNINGS

The surprising facts as disclosed from the media sources quoted above show Mukesh to be a grounded person, living a simple life. He may be surrounded by wealth and maybe he splurges occasionally, but his lifestyle is still simple. He still works hard when he could choose to lead a life of luxury and enjoy his wealth.

He had grown up amidst hardship and had witnessed the growth along with his family members. His childhood days were spent in a unique combination of learning under perhaps the best teacher ever, his father Dhirubhai, coupled with the practical experience of Mahendrabhai, a teacher who would come to their home to teach, alongside his formal education. This probably gave the Ambani siblings a well-rounded education of not only the academic world but also exposed them to the realities of life, which sometimes are not always available for the next generation. If you think about it, we as parents often deprive our children of learning experiences or do our best to prevent them from learning about failures or disappointments, since we would like them to avoid facing the hardships that we may have faced. This prevents them from learning how to handle disappointments and failure. Thus, they usually grow up with an unrealistic view of how they perceive the world. Normally, this is an issue that most parents grapple with and hence, we see multiple cases of the next generation growing up with a sense of entitlement or arrogance; or maybe with insecurities and complexes. But this was not the case with the Ambani family, as Dhirubhai, in his wisdom, had raised his children in such a manner that the core values were transferred and there was a sense of being grounded along with appreciation for hard work.

Contrary to what most people may think, the move into plastics was not just a coincidence. Mukesh studied chemical engineering but has stated that he moved to plastics and textiles inspired by the movie *The Graduate,* where the hero was advised to move into plastics!

Another inspiring thought is the fact that Mukesh moved to the site where the plant was being set up. Not as an owner, but practically as one of the team members and was hands-on! This shows that the commitment and dedication was inherent right from the very beginning. This also brings out his willingness to get his hands dirty and be involved with the grass-roots level of a project. This quality did help him immensely in his later years, since he had a very good understanding of the projects that he was executing.

His skills were built on setting up the Reliance plants from the time that he joined Reliance, hence he had a very close connection with the company. The statement made by him, about him being treated as a first-generation partner instead of a second-generation inheritor, is very interesting.

Let us try to understand this statement. There are various sayings, in various countries around the world that are usually found in family businesses (and this has been backed by research) that most businesses do not last beyond three generations. The sayings state that the first generation creates the family business, the second maintains it and the third is not able to preserve it and ends up destroying it. The fact that Mukesh has been working with his father, shows his level of involvement and commitment to the family business. It also reflects how closely he identifies himself with the business as an entrepreneur who has founded the business, rather than just as a second-generation inheritor. This could explain the drive and the passion that Mukesh has shown while at the helm of Reliance. He has been setting an example for all, by pushing himself and working hard.

Persevere and Prevail Like Mukesh Ambani

If one looks at the growth of Reliance, one can see that it has grown by providing solutions to some of the most acute issues facing India. Reliance has been able to achieve rapid growth by providing these solutions. The textile era had registered hyper-growth at a time when cotton fabrics were not able to meet the demand of the growing population and synthetic fibres like polyester would have helped meet the demand at a lower cost. The high volumes of Reliance helped increase the availability along with affordability, much more than what cotton fabrics could ever have achieved.

Mukesh's refinery and oil exploration venture was in response to India's high energy needs. His retail venture is supposed to help the Indian farmers, with their produce being sold in the Reliance stores, thus supposedly cutting out the tier of middlemen, who have historically been controlling the supply chain.

His tendency to learn from his children and adapt accordingly is a powerful indicator of his humility and openness to newer facts. In spite of his success and multiple achievements, he has not let that go to his head. He is not biased towards all that he knows, he is willing to accept the fact that his knowledge may not be adequate and that the world may have changed. He reads so that he builds up his knowledge of what he does not know, so instead of living in denial and refusing to accept change, he chooses to understand the change. He learns how to exploit the opportunities that the new environment offers and makes his moves to profit from these. And he does this on a scale, which to most would appear foolish and scary. He does not care about what competitors may think, he just steamrolls ahead and succeeds.

2
MUKESH AMBANI'S MANAGEMENT STYLE

Look to the future, use high technology, integrate along the value chain and go for large scale.[28]

Mukesh Ambani got his first experience at managing a business independently when he was asked to supervise the setting up of the Patalganga

---

[28]ECN, 'Reliance Industries pushes to complete Jamnagar refinery', www.icis.com, 22 July 2007, accessed 9 August 2019, https://www.icis.com/explore/resources/news/2007/07/23/9046296/reliance-industries-pushes-to-complete-jamnagar-refinery/

refinery. He was told to build the business from scratch, without taking anyone from Reliance. But he was a quick learner and quickly made his mark, proving himself. He had to learn quickly because, in spite of his degree in chemical engineering, he hardly had any hands-on practical experience. His core team was very small and he had some support from the established and experienced managers in other parts of the company. His company started to get a US-centric focus during his time for the reasons covered below. He started to adopt professional standards, starting with recruitment. He ensured that every recruit had not only the professional qualifications and experience, but was also professionally vetted. He disliked the Indian bureaucratic systems and structures and worked to introduce US-style management thoughts and practices in their daily management processes. To cite one example, he insisted that all meetings and communication within the project team be conducted face-to-face. This also included meetings with the contractors![29]

---

[29]Kannan Ramaswamy, 'Reliance Industries: An Indian family business come of age in global energy and petrochemicals', Thunderbird School of Global Management, 2012

FOCUS ON WORLD MARKETS AND SCALE[30]

Mukesh followed Dhirubhai's philosophy of large-scale facilities. He was not concerned about the local capacities and demand, and set up plants which were at times making far more than the total domestic demand in India! He had set his sights on the international markets and wanted to cater to those markets globally, rather than restrict his focus to the local domestic protected markets.

SETTING UP PROCESSES TO REDUCE THE DEPENDENCE ON A FEW INDIVIDUALS[31]

One of the major changes he made was to change the management style then prevailing at the company. He saw that the experts (he called them 'heroes') came in with information that only they had access to, with their notes containing various readings of different process conditions, which they referred to and carried

---

[30]Sucheta Dalal and Debashis Basu, 'The arbitrage in farm produce is much bigger than that in software services: Mukesh Ambani', Moneylife.in, 13 April 2010, accessed 15 August 2019, https://www.moneylife.in/article/the-arbitrage-in-farm-produce-is-much-bigger-than-that-in-software-services-mukesh-ambani/4744.html
[31]Ibid.

back with them. Mukesh realized that this behaviour would come in the path of their growth and they had to change that style. And hence, he started to work on a more open environment where one had Standard Operating Procedures (SOPs) and Standard Operating Conditions (SOCs), which aligned everyone and thus everyone could contribute to it. Thereby the business was not dependent on a few managers who were 'carrying their wisdom in their notebooks as if it is some kind of secretive operation.'[32]

BUY THE BEST TECHNOLOGY

Mukesh talks about the time when he took over and found that the competition was buying licences for amounts ranging between half a million to one million dollars. In this situation, Mukesh agreed to pay DuPont $5 million for their licence, since he wanted to work with the best. He got a few experts from DuPont and then put a few 25-year-olds to learn from them the operations and how to sustain the chemical processes. This trait of collaborating with the best is a common thread throughout his future years also, when he had various kinds of tie-ups, alliances and agreements

---

[32]Ibid.

with the likes of British Petroleum, DuPont, Bechtel, Samsung, LG and a host of retail brands.[33]

FOCUS ON ATTRACTING YOUNG TALENT[34]

Mukesh built a team of new managers, drawn from his family and friends, including his classmates from his college days. He also built up a team of professionals, including attracting overseas Indians who wanted to return home. The pool of talent also included experienced professionals from reputed competitors in Europe and the US, along with toppers from the best engineering colleges in India. Mukesh also ensured that, in his initial days, once the deals were signed, he assigned many young engineers to the project, so that they could capture the knowledge early on and this would provide them with a potentially huge advantage in their career. He also obsessed with creating an environment where the senior management gave the younger 25-year-old managers, opportunities to make meaningful contributions.[35]

---

[33]Kannan Ramaswamy, 'Reliance Industries: Building Execution Excellence in an Emerging Market', Teaching Case, TB0517, Thunderbird School of Global Management, 2018
[34]Ibid.
[35]Kannan Ramaswamy, 'Reliance Industries: An Indian family

Reliance Industries Limited (RIL), under Mukesh, in 2010, wanted to transform human resources to build a world-class organization which would attract a much younger workforce (the 2010 average workforce age was 41 years). Mukesh worked on developing innovative talent and used human resources effectively by incorporating the commonly known concepts of performance management, transparency, rewards and recognition, and effective succession planning.[36] By 2019, RIL had 194,056 employees, with over 48.8 per cent below the age of 30.[37]

BENCHMARK USING GLOBAL EXPERTS

Mukesh had used the US global giants to benchmark his operations. He had stated that he was inspired by large US chemical companies such as DuPont. He appreciated the openness of the US company, from which he learnt significantly. He took advantage of the open society and the fact that one could get standards, data, etc. from the (sic) U.S. Association of Chemical Engineers. Information was relatively difficult to get

---

business comes of age in global energy and petrochemicals', Thunderbird School of Global Management, 2012
[36] Ibid.
[37] Reliance Annual Report 2018–19, page 120.

at that time, compared to current times, when the Internet makes getting access to information a lot easier. Sometimes, the information needed came at a cost, but Mukesh feels that it was worth the investment to get the proper structure and direction to their thought processes.[38]

FOCUS ON SAFETY

Mukesh also focussed on safety culture within the company, along with the SOPs and SOCs. RIL learnt its early safety culture from its partners, Bechtel and DuPont, and to drive this point further, RIL started working specifically with contractors and suppliers who had a reputation for safety. It asked DuPont and Shell for help in conducting external audits of its safety performance every year. RIL rolled out an extensive Health, Safety, and Environment Management System (HSE-MS). This system launched an annual reporting system in 2004 and covered all areas of its operations. The annual reports were designed on the lines of the reports by global corporations. They reported

---

[38]Kannan Ramaswamy, 'Reliance Industries: An Indian family business comes of age in global energy and petrochemicals', Thunderbird School of Global Management, 2012

data on RIL's performance on important criteria like occupational safety, training and development of its employees, its social commitments and its environmental performance track record. These guidelines were not just internally set standards but were based on the safety standards set by international bodies like the British Safety Council and the American Society for Training and Development (ASTD). Soon, RIL started to consistently win awards for its safety performance and safety innovations from these global institutions, as well as local bodies such as the Institution of Engineers (India), Indian Merchants' Chamber and the Ministry of Petroleum and Natural Gas. These included the HSE Award-Platinum category for the year 2017–2018 and the Platinum Award for outstanding achievement in the field of Environment Management in Textile Sector at the 18th Annual Greentech Environment Award 2018, to name a few.[39]

TIE-UP WITH GLOBAL EXPERTS

Mukesh believed in tying up with the best for global expertise. We have seen earlier that he had preferred

---

[39] Kannan Ramaswamy, 'Reliance Industries: Building Execution Excellence in an Emerging Market', Teaching Case, TB0517, Thunderbird School of Global Management, 2018

to buy the technology from DuPont for the Patalganga refinery, but he continued this trend throughout his entrepreneurial journey.

BRITISH PETROLEUM (BP)

In August 2019, he announced at the Reliance AGM, that RIL would be setting up a joint venture with British Petroleum (BP), with Reliance holding 51 per cent and the balance being held by BP.

The joint venture would set up 5,500 fuel retail stations and would include RIL's present 1,378 retail outlets, which RIL was running independently across India. This joint venture would also market aviation turbine fuel for the Indian aviation industry and would include RIL's aviation fuel business. RIL, at the time, had a presence in over 30 airports across India.[40] The agreement was subject to regulatory and other customary approvals and is expected to be completed by the first half of 2020. The joint venture is expected to benefit from access to a competitive fuel supply

---

[40]Kalpana Pathak, 'Reliance-BP ink new fuel retail JV: to set up 5,500 petrol pump outlets in 5 years', Livemint, 6 August 2019, accessed 14 August 2019, https://www.livemint.com/companies/news/ril-bp-ink-new-fuel-retail-jv-to-set-up-5-500-petrol-pump-outlets-in-5-years-1565092419894.html

from RIL's Jamnagar refinery. It was in October 2016, that BP had received a licence to set up 3,500 fuel outlets in India, and earlier in January 2016, got the licence to market jet fuel (or aviation turbine fuel [ATF]) in India. RIL held a licence to set up 5,000 fuel retail outlets and had plans to double its market share of the fuel retail segment, which was 7 to 8 per cent at that time.[41]

Earlier, RIL had also tied up with BP for exploration and production, when in February 2011, BP had bought a 30 per cent stake in 21 oil and gas production-sharing contracts which were operated by RIL for an amount of $7.2 billion.[42]

In another media report in August 2019, it was stated that RIL and BP Plc would invest ₹5,000 crores in bringing three sets of natural gas fields in the Krishna Godavari basin block in the Bay of Bengal,

---

[41]'Reliance and BP to create major world-class fuels partnership for India's fast-growing market', Green Car Congress, 9 August 2019 accessed 14 August 2019, https://www.greencarcongress.com/2019/08/20190809-india.html

[42]Kalpana Pathak, 'Reliance-BP ink new fuel retail JV: to set up 5,500 petrol pump outlets in 5 years', Livemint, 6 August 2019, accessed 14 August 2019, https://www.livemint.com/companies/news/ril-bp-ink-new-fuel-retail-jv-to-set-up-5-500-petrol-pump-outlets-in-5-years-1565092419894.html

to production[43]. This was supposed to help increase the gas output which was at the time falling. The gas block was at one time the largest gas-producing block in the country. The investment sanction for this joint venture was announced in India that year. The projects to develop these gas fields were amongst the most complex being executed anywhere in the world.[44]

BP and RIL also have an equal partnership in the joint venture company, India Gas Solutions Pvt. Ltd, which was set up for sourcing and marketing of gas in India.[45]

FOCUS ON EXECUTING PLANS TO THE LAST DETAIL

Mukesh is known to execute his plans down to the minutest detail. He can execute hugely complex projects,

---

[43] ANI, 'Reliance, BP joint venture to invest Rs 35,000 crore in KG basin', *The Economic Times*, 12 August 2019

[44] ANI, 'Reliance, BP joint venture to invest Rs 35,000 crore in KG basin', *The Economic Times*, 12 August 2019, accessed 16 August 2019, https://economictimes.indiatimes.com/industry/energy/oil-gas/reliance-bp-joint-venture-to-invest-rs-35000-crore-in-kg-basin/articleshow/70645776.cms

[45] Kalpana Pathak, 'Reliance-BP ink new fuel retail JV: to set up 5,500 petrol pump outlets in 5 years', Livemint, 6 August 2019, accessed 14 August 2019, https://www.livemint.com/companies/news/ril-bp-ink-new-fuel-retail-jv-to-set-up-5-500-petrol-pump-outlets-in-5-years-1565092419894.html

before time and under cost. Some people say, perhaps apocryphally, that the delay in launching Reliance Jio Infocomm Limited (Jio) was due to his insistence on getting every problem sorted out to perfection so that the service would work very efficiently right from day one.

Many claim that the success of Reliance has been due to political lobbying, something which many firms in India do, and that Reliance is unmatched in its ability to get laws modified in its favour and protecting itself from external scrutiny.[46] These have been dismissed by Mukesh as 'fables' and he is stated to have said that this is not a critical success factor.

However, he recalls that his children were quite blunt in their questioning of his being in the plastics business, which was not really an environmental-friendly industry. (Though one has to admit, that, as per their annual reports, being environmental-friendly has been an area that Reliance has been proactive on. They appreciated the size of the business, but they also called on him to re-evaluate his portfolio, which he did with amusement stating, that with billions of dollars

---

[46] Anand Giridharadas, 'Indian to the Core, and an Oligarch', *The New York Times*, New York edition, 15 June 2008, accessed 15 August 2019, https://www.nytimes.com/2008/06/15/business/worldbusiness/15ambani.html

invested in plastics, it may have been a little late. But given the steps taken by him in recent years, such as investing in retail and Jio and his move to chemicals, he may have shown some inclination to follow that advice of diversifying his portfolio.[47]

JIO PROJECT IDEA

The idea was conceived when his daughter Isha was home for her holidays and she commented that she was unable to submit her homework online, as the 'the Internet sucks'. This led to the idea which eventually became Jio.

Jio was the second time that Mukesh entered the mobile telecom industry; the first venture was handed over to his younger brother post the split a few years ago.

The Jio project started with Mukesh writing a 36-page handwritten memo to his executives in December 2010. These notes were scanned and emailed to some executives by him. The notes described the telecom venture's potential in great technical detail. This memo detailed his plans which were the origins of what would later become Jio.

---

[47] Ibid.

According to *The Wall Street Journal*, the memo detailed out a 4G (fourth-generation) wireless service with '99.999 per cent' network availability, 'integration with an app store, ours or others' to help smartphone users order fast food or buy movie tickets, sourcing of mobile devices from China and Taiwan, content delivery to 'three screens': cell phones, laptops and TVs, and two 300,000 square-foot data centres.[48] There was an estimate of 60,000 cell towers and another page had complex mathematical calculations of how fast each cell tower could carry data.

The notes also mentioned the features that Reliance wanted to explore getting into, such as social networking platform and education platforms. The data centres would be used to host remote cloud-based web services for businesses. It mentioned the need to 'co-create and innovate with device vendors to come up with LTE vendors'. (TD-LTE was the 4G technology that Reliance was using. It was not the standard in the US or Europe, so global smartphone makers were not making devices for the technology as yet.)

One anecdote indicates the deep level of detailed

---

[48]Amol Sharma and Megha Bahree, 'In India, Dreaming of A 4G World', *The Wall Street Journal*, 25 July 2011, accessed 15 August 2019, https://www.wsj.com/articles/SB10000872396390443295404 5775470022646000084

thought that they go into while executing. While rolling out Jio, Reliance had to lay down a huge network of high-tech optical fibres network across India. There was always the threat of theft and hence, subsequent break down of the network. The challenge of thieves seeking out copper cables for the copper was also prevalent. The Reliance fibre was just a thin mostly plastic cable of probably no resale value, hence of no interest to such thieves.[49]

So what did they do?

Reliance hired an army quite literally! They hired and made teams of security personnel who were ex-army staff, tasked with the responsibility of looking after the Reliance lines. RIL also left a few feet of spare cable coiled on top of the manhole covers, so that the thieves looking for copper, could see that the cable was made of mostly plastic materials and hence, not worth pulling out. The company also hired locals who were paid to keep an eye out for any problems![50] Simple local solutions for problems!

---

[49]Newley Purnell, 'Two Years Ago, India Lacked Fast, Cheap Internet—One Billionaire Changed All That', *The Wall Street Journal*, 5 September 2018, accessed 15 August 2019, https://www.wsj.com/articles/two-years-ago-india-lacked-fast-cheap-Internetone-billionaire-changed-all-that-1536159916?mod=e2tw
[50]Ibid.

In August 2019, Mukesh announced his plans for Jio. One of the most sensational service offerings was the First Day First Show, to be launched in mid-2020, in which he had stated that the Premium Jio customers would be able to see movies on the very first day of their release in the theatres![51] This had a huge impact on the share prices of the theatrical movie distributors who saw a dip in their stock prices![52]

LEARNINGS

The story of Reliance today, is the story of the fast execution of huge projects at world-beating costs. If there is one significant factor which has been the hallmark of Mukesh's audacious ability to have a grand vision, it is his ability to actually execute it, within time and often below cost!

---

[51]Business FP Staff, 'RIL AGM 2019 Updates: Reliance Industries aims to become zero net-debt company in next 18 months: Mukesh Always', *Firstpost* online, 12 August 2019, accessed 23 September 2019, https://www.firstpost.com/business/ril-agm-2019-live-all-eyes-on-mukesh-ambanis-speech-groups-plans-for-jio-e-commerce-expected-7147441.html

[52]Pallavi Pengonda, 'PVR, Inox shares recover post RIL shock, but winter may be coming', 19 August 2019, accessed 23 September 2019, https://www.livemint.com/market/mark-to-market/pvr-inox-shares-recover-post-ril-shock-but-winter-may-be-coming-1566237945096.html

His ability to put in processes to remove the dependence on certain key people helped him to ensure that the company grew and was not held back due to the insecurities of a few. He also encouraged the younger talent to take up more responsibilities, by giving them larger roles and more learning opportunities.

His preference to tie up with world leaders is also suggestive of a smart and visionary strategy. By choosing a proven vendor, perhaps the best in the world, he was assured of the product quality and their ability to deliver. This probably reduced costs and uncertainty in commissioning time. Additionally, to get good people and pay them well are ways of ensuring the employee turnover is low.

Mukesh was working on large-scale projects, some of which were actually on a scale unseen before in the world. And he wanted to execute them flawlessly. His choice of world-class experts, virtually guaranteed that the best brains and experience were working on the projects and that the chances of success were probably highest in that respect. This ensured that he was able to save on quick execution in spite of whatever extra costs he incurred in choosing the best vendors.

The need for processes and SOPs was created to reduce the power of the managers. These managers held on to the process knowledge and this prevented others from learning. We find that this practice still prevails in most organizations, where the older employees still resort to this, as they are insecure. Holding back the knowledge to themselves, in their opinion, gives them job security, as they think that they will be retained as long they are indispensable. This does not make organizations grow, as one needs to have people who can step in, in case of absenteeism or any other reason and additionally, one cannot promote or retire these people since they have not trained any replacements who can take their place. So the entire business suffers.

Mukesh realized this and by introducing the SOPs, took the power away from these hoarders of knowledge. It is very important for the workers on the factory floor to be well-versed with the information on operating processes if the organization has to grow and succeed. Any growing business needs to have well-trained and knowledgeable personnel. Additionally, having well-trained people in adequate numbers ensures that there is always another person to take the place in case one is promoted or leaves the organization.

The focus on safety demonstrates his ability and willingness to learn something new from others outside the company and reflects on what would work for his company. Reflecting on these new aspects and then adapting these within Reliance demonstrate his willingness and hunger for learning newer practices, as per what the foreign technology partners or competitors were doing, and thereby, implementing an improved but modified version within his organization. This example offers an interesting management lesson.

Usually, most leaders try to reinvent the wheel and work tirelessly on implementing various processes within their organizations. But more often than not, these would have probably already been solved in some manner in some other firms, maybe by the leading company in the same industry or in some other industry. Leaders can observe what is being carried on in other companies and try to adapt the measures taken by these companies to employ within their businesses, instead of starting from a clean slate every time. This will lead to quicker and maybe more relevant solutions which can be set to work immediately, instead of experimenting, which often fails. Though failure by itself is not bad, it is time-consuming to find out what works. Additionally, one could also learn from the best practices of other companies who may have put into practice, processes to avoid the mistakes that they had made earlier. Usually, this knowledge can be used across industries. For example, Mukesh learnt about safety from his partners, Bechtel and DuPont.

Mukesh Ambani's Management Style

Choosing good partners who have the experience and the expertise gives one the advantage to scale up faster and go a lot farther. Reliance has typically preferred to go alone with its audaciously huge projects, preferring to buy out technology and hire the best talent, whatever the cost. In my opinion, the tie-ups then seem to be reserved for those areas where it did not think it profitable to invest on its own or that it may have made more commercial sense to partner up. Various other newspaper reports have also stated that the tie-ups could also be seen as an opportunity for Reliance to unlock value and cash out some of the valuations that it has built up. Whatever point of view one may consider, the fact remains that either way it makes sense for Reliance and shows the depth behind Mukesh's thought process.

The tie-ups with BP indicate that RIL was tying up with the oil major, as BP probably had the experience to extract oil from a complex project like the Krishna Godavari Dhirubhai 6 (KG-D6) block, given that BP had long been operating in the choppy and difficult environment of the North Sea.

The Jio notes (which *The Wall Street Journal* writes about) indicate the detailed thought Mukesh goes into, before diving into a project. For a project of this magnitude, which eventually went on to invest billions of dollars, we can see that Mukesh has first put in a lot of thought into every minute aspect of the business. This has been the basis for Jio's successful roll-out. The learning from this is that managers should plan their future moves in as much detail as possible. Most managers rush in to invest in new projects, based on whatever is the flavour of the month or on what the other competitors are investing in, without thinking much of the consequences or the potential of the new business. This often leads to failures or maybe in case of multiple entrants, senseless price wars which lead to low profitability for most players, with some players choosing to exit or close down. Some managers may question the wisdom of planning in an uncertain environment, which could mean that the best laid out plans could become redundant, but as Dwight Eisenhower had been quoted as saying, 'Plans are worthless, planning is everything'. The exercise of but planning helps to start work smartly, even if it means that the first thing that you may have to do is to discard the plans made earlier. The process of planning helps one think and hence, draw up fresh plans much faster than in a case where there was no process of planning done earlier. In this manner, leaders and entrepreneurs are better prepared to face the vagaries of a fast-changing environment.

Mukesh Ambani's Management Style

Reliance found a local solution and not a high-tech one to the challenge that it faced. When most managers face challenges, they usually think that resorting to technology or more expensive solutions would help, but it may not always serve the purpose. Sometimes simple solutions based on the context (or the environment) could serve to solve the challenge or be better than what the most complex technological solution may offer. Managers are advised to consider all options including the simple, effective ones, which are relevant to their environments in which they operate, before deciding on any option.

A family business owner once stated to me, that he could not grow as he had a retail outlet and he felt that only his family members could be trusted to handle the cash. I asked him, what other industries are in the retail sector and how have they handled this challenge? So, we looked at luxury retail outlets, jewellery chain stores, etc. to see how they have grown, and what systems they had put in place. The next step was to go even further, to those organizations that by definition handle cash, such as banks, foreign exchange dealers, temples, etc. and see what systems and processes they had installed. This gave a good starting point to this family business leader to start thinking of what he could do in his organization. Needless to say, he had enough food for thought to start executing changes within his company!

Wise leadership need not reinvent everything within their firm, but just observe others who may have already solved the same challenge. Also, look for indicators of what factors the other leading companies are addressing and consider if this is something that you should also be working on, and adopt it if required.

3

WHAT ARE THE BIGGEST LEARNINGS FOR MUKESH AMBANI?

In February 2019, at Nasscom Foundation's annual leadership summit in Mumbai, Mukesh was asked about his biggest learning.[53]

According to Mukesh, he had learnt his lessons the hard way, by experience and from his father, in school

---

[53] Masoom Gupte, 'Entrepreneurs, take heed! Here are Mukesh Ambani's 5 career lessons', *The Economic Times*, 24 February 2019, accessed 17 August 2019, https://economictimes.indiatimes.com/magazines/panache/entrepreneurs-take-heed-here-are-mukesh-ambanis-5-career-lessons/articleshow/57321703.cms

and from his teacher, who taught him life. Besides these four, his other learnings were as follows.

The first learning came from his father when Mukesh had returned from Stanford University. He had asked his father what his job was going to be and what he had to do. His father, Dhirubhai, had stated that only managers would seek out a job with clearly defined roles and responsibilities. On the other hand, entrepreneurs would figure out what they want to do. And with that, Dhirubhai further stated that he would not tell Mukesh anything and left it to Mukesh to figure out what he wanted to do.

The second learning was, as an entrepreneur, to find a problem that one is passionate about, to solve. This was a lesson he learnt from his teacher in UDCT, which is equally relevant for entrepreneurs. The teacher had said that he (the teacher) would not grade his students on a prepared list of problems to be solved. Instead, the grading was on the quality of problems that the students found out and the quality of the solutions offered by them. Mukesh feels that similarly, entrepreneurs need not just solve a problem, but they need to find the problem first. And then, once they have found it, they need to solve it. Additionally, the problem needs to be one which helps society. Solving societies' needs has to be the main objective of the business, not just financial returns. He felt that one cannot become great by focussing only on the returns.

The third learning is to accept and learn from failures. One should not get disappointed by failures. He gave his example and said that he had failed on many occasions before becoming successful. Failures should be treated as a step towards success. One should not be disheartened by failure but learn from them and never give up.

The next learning was to figure out what the non-negotiables are for an entrepreneur. Mukesh said that two of his non-negotiables were, to treat the investor's money more carefully than his own and the second was to have the right A-team, which is aligned to his passion. He felt that one could never achieve anything without these.

Lastly the need to be positive and an optimist, as the entrepreneur will face many cynics and negative people, yet he/she needs to spread positive energy and move on.

LEARNINGS

The above is very simple and clear, needing no explanation. But I would be failing in my objectives if

I did not add some additional comments to reinforce this understanding.

Dhirubhai's words to Mukesh and the above lessons represent, to some extent, the essence of what is taught in entrepreneurship today.

An entrepreneur today creates an opportunity out of a need. He is driven by the passion for making a difference, helping make the world a better place and this passion drives the entrepreneur in his determination to achieve. It is this obsession that keeps them going.

So, when one reads the lines which Dhirubhai said to Mukesh, it is echoing this same sentiment which defines an entrepreneur. Most entrepreneurs who have succeeded in a big way have started out with a common problem faced by society—one which was not addressed with a practical and sustainable solution. We need to be more open to finding problems AND solving them. I write the 'and' in bold, to emphasize that it is up to us to find the solutions for challenges that we or others face. Merely identifying the problem and leaving it unsolved and complaining about it, does not help anyone. The biggest opportunities are those challenges which most people have accepted as a way of life and have got used to facing regularly. So, when one offers a solution, it becomes quickly accepted, especially if it removes a pain point and makes customers' life easier, at an affordable price.

Another point could be of selecting the problems that one wants to solve. This becomes a self-selecting effort, as an entrepreneur would work towards causes that he feels most passionate about. Hence, it is very important to find what causes one wants to work on/for and focus on those.

Of course, solving society's problems is a noble objective to follow, with many entrepreneurs finding great success in doing so. Others have made their fortunes in pursuits which may have created more problems than necessarily solving them, but generally, businesses which can solve problems and contribute to social benefits are more sustainable in the longer term. The key aspect to be kept in mind is that the ventures should be profitable so that the business is sustainable.

The need to be positive and to have certain non-negotiables is also a good learning for entrepreneurs. There are many challenges/hurdles in the path of entrepreneurship, where the entrepreneur may be tested and forced to make compromises, and thus, having clarity on what is a non-negotiable is an invaluable guidepost in making decisions.

Entrepreneurs may have to face many obstacles and rejections in their path, they may not taste success early on, (or at all, in some cases!) and it does help to keep a positive outlook. This helps overcome obstacles and keep on working towards success.

4
TIME AS A COMPETITIVE ADVANTAGE: LEARN THE VALUE OF TIME

The hallmark of any project under Mukesh Ambani has been fast execution and the breaking of world records in the commissioning of projects.

Mukesh, while setting up the Patalganga refinery, deviated from the standard norms.[54] Usually in projects, it's a common practice to invite bids from

---

[54]Kannan Ramaswamy, 'Reliance Industries: An Indian family business comes of age in global energy and petrochemicals', Teaching case, Thunderbird School of Global Management, 2012

various contractors for various components of the project, according to the work defined by the buyer. Based on this, usually, the lowest offer is accepted.

Mukesh went against this practice. He preferred to instead award contracts to those companies who had bid sometimes two to three times more than the lowest price offered by others!

Why did he do this?

The answer which seems simple and obvious shows the genius in his thinking process. He awarded them the contracts based on their record of having executed earlier projects. Mukesh wanted to complete his project fast and hence, speed and competency were critical.

The result?

The Patalganga petrochemical project was finished in 18 months and the commercial production started in 1982.

A DuPont executive had stated that the same project would have taken at least 26 months to go online in any developed country![55]

Another anecdote comes from the time of Dhirubhai and the commissioning of the Patalganga plant. Most companies would normally wait for the

---

[55]Ibid.

equipment to land after which they would link it to the various pieces through the large network of pipes that are normally seen in any petrochemical complex. The Ambanis did something unique. They laid down the pipes in readiness for the equipment. And this was somewhere near 220 km of pipes. The plant was installed in between the pipes as and when the machinery was delivered![56]

LEARNINGS

The biggest learning from any Reliance project under Mukesh is the value of time in executing projects. He preferred to spend money on higher priced, better contractors if it meant setting up his projects faster.

This is a very important aspect, where time has been taken as the central resource. Normally, in management, one is taught that one needs to optimize the financial resources (that is, save money to the extent possible) and execute the project in the most cost-effective manner. This method attempts to save money, as it assumes that money (or capital) is a scarce resource. But this would mean that the time taken to execute the project would be longer.

---

[56]Ibid.

Mukesh's thought process is based on the assumption that money is not in short supply, but time is. The thinking is that if one can reduce the time spent on setting up a project and execute it fast, they can recover by production in the time saved whatever extra money they have spent in its commissioning. Hence, one must spend the maximum sums of money needed to save on time and ensure quick execution. Hence his logic was that one should spend to get projects done well in time.

This time-based project execution had its genesis in two areas that Reliance considered its strengths: the ability to quantify the tasks involved in a complex project and its ability to get huge resources to complete the tasks. The rationale, as explained by one key personnel in Reliance, was that they (Reliance) place the largest amount of resources that a particular task can absorb, without getting in anyone's way. The issue of optimization (that is, saving money by cost-cutting) would arise if there was unlimited time. But not in current-day scenarios, where mostly we do not calculate how much production we have lost due to delays in the completion of the projects. Hence, leaders can consider spending a little more on project execution, if it means faster commissioning. This way, they can gain an advantage if one can get the production going earlier. Reliance had discovered that one gets a more accurate estimate of the cost of any project when they also included the value of time, in their cost calculations. And they could conclude in all such calculations, that at all times, it made a lot of sense to spend the maximum amounts of resources on a task (saturate a task with resources to the maximum extent it can absorb) to complete it faster.[57]

Leaders should think about this logic, which is a little contrary in view, but has a lot of wisdom. We often see delays and cost overruns being the norm in most projects and the cost of lost production is usually not considered while the project is being planned. This becomes even more important in current times when capital is no longer the constraint it was in the 1980s.

---

[57] K.K. Malhotra, head of manufacturing, in Kannan Ramaswamy, 'Reliance Industries: An Indian family business comes of age in global energy and petrochemicals', Teaching case, Thunderbird School of Global Management, 2012

5
FLEXIBILITY AND INTEGRATION OF THE VALUE CHAIN

The oil refining process is complex, to put it in very simple, non-technical terms. It involves crude as an input and the output is various petro-products like diesel, petrol or chemicals. Depending on how one designs the refinery and what processes one builds into the refinery, one can produce certain output products. The type of outputs one can produce depends on the processes that one has built into the refinery. This is called the complexity index, which is covered later in this book. Most refineries worldwide are set up to make

Flexibility and Integration of the Value Chain

a particular level of complexity and can make a range of products, using a certain range of input products.

Mukesh Ambani has built his plants with a great degree of flexibility. This may have resulted in the initial plant costs shooting up, as compared to their competitors, but it has also given Reliance the flexibility to operate on a much larger range of quality of raw materials (crude oil). At the same time, it gives him the option to decide what finished goods are the most profitable. This way, he can reduce his raw material costs, and at the same time, decide to make the most profitable mix of finished products. Additionally, with the high efficiencies in plant operations, he has also managed to get the lowest costs of operations.

On this basis, the Jamnagar plant has the option for multiple types of crude oil and can manufacture different types of expensive fuels and products as output. This gives it the flexibility to decide what type of raw materials to buy and what products to produce.

In reality, the Reliance game plan to maximize profits had started very early on, right from Dhirubhai's time. At that time, Reliance followed a backward integration strategy, when it went further upstream to get the assured supplies of raw materials and at the same time, get higher margins, in a competitive market. Initially, the Reliance footprint expanded in many locations, with new facilities being set up in Hazira, Patalganga and Jamnagar. The backward integration for the polyester filament yarn-textile chain was established in Patalganga, with new installations being set up for manufacturing linear alkyl benzene (LAB) and paraxylene, an input for manufacturing purified terephthalic acid (PTA).[58]

In 1992, additional investments were done in Hazira port in Gujarat to set up a new industrial complex for the manufacture of monoethylene glycol (MEG), polyvinyl chloride (PVC), ethylene oxide and subsequently, high-density polyethylene (HDPE). This complex was also designed after a lot of careful planning and having considered future pricing trends in the global markets for feedstock and end products. The key feature of this complex was its flexibility in its ability to switch, at short notice, from manufacturing HDPE to linear low-density polyethylene (LLDPE). It also could permit usage of multiple feedstocks such as liquefied natural gas (LNG), naphtha or gas liquids. This would give it a very wide range of possibilities to choose its inputs and outputs, to suit the then-

---

[58]Kannan Ramaswamy, 'Reliance Industries: An Indian family business comes of age in global energy and petrochemicals', Teaching case, Thunderbird School of Global Management, 2012

prevailing fuel price conditions and be able to quickly respond to market changes.[59]

Mukesh has chosen to change his strategy to suit the environment and to keep this company sustainable for the future. The Reliance strategy traditionally had been based on oil, petroleum products and plastics. These commodities comprise almost 74 per cent of the earnings before interest, tax, depreciation and amortization (EBITDA) of ₹78,184 crore in Financial Year (FY) 2018.[60] Though Mukesh had stated that in 2019, he expected his two new businesses, retail and telecom, to contribute as much as the energy and petrochemical businesses to the overall earnings of the company.

To explain this better, as can be seen above, the traditional strategy that Reliance followed in its businesses was that of backward integration, where RIL started as a yarn trader and then became a textile manufacturer. Thereafter, under Dhirubhai's visionary leadership, RIL moved upstream (backwards) entering the polymers business, followed by petrochemicals,

---

[59] Ibid.
[60] Aveek Datta, 'Mukesh Ambani seeks to future-proof RIL', *Fortune India* online, 7 July 2018, accessed 28 July 2019, https://www.fortuneindia.com/enterprise/mukesh-ambani-seeks-to-future-proof-ril/102103

oil refining and then finally production of crude. This strategy was a classic backward integration strategy where a company moves its scope of activities to cover increasingly larger economies of scale and get increased margins. This step also ensures that the company gets its raw materials securely without having to depend on external vendors.

This strategy of integrating backwards enabled the company to work with lower costs and higher volumes. This was something that RIL did quite successfully, with Jamnagar becoming amongst the largest refineries in a single location in the world. Typically, those companies that would like to follow this model would invest in huge capacities and then try to produce as much as possible, to reduce their operating costs still further.

Reliance used this strategy very effectively during the time of Dhirubhai, who put up capacities in India which were more than the total demand!

The Reliance strategy, right from the time of Dhirubhai, has been driven by two factors—to focus on quality and to control the value chain.[61]

It was also this strategy that propelled Dhirubhai to move from trading to manufacturing when he

---

[61] Kannan Ramaswamy, 'Reliance Industries: An Indian Family business comes of age in global energy and petrochemicals', Teaching Case TB 0303, Thunderbird School of Global Management, 2012. Page 2

Flexibility and Integration of the Value Chain

set up a spinning mill using borrowed funds. It was established at a tenth of the cost which a competitor paid to acquire a similar mill at the time.[62] And this was before Reliance went public in 1977.

This led to RIL integrating backwards into manufacturing synthetic yarn fabrics which used polyester filament yarn (PFY) and polyester staple fibre (PSF) as raw materials. This was also helped to some extent by a change in the government policy which allowed preferential imports of PFY and PSF to those companies exporting synthetic fabrics. The company adopted the latest technology, fuelled by Dhirubhai's desire to be competitive with other countries such as Japan, Korea, and Taiwan. RIL started importing technologies which would help it grow fast and it used the export market demand to fuel its rapid growth. The growing export sales gave it import entitlement privileges, which it used to import the most sophisticated and latest technology to improve its capacities and quality still further. It did not give any dividends choosing instead to invest in growing its business. Its sales doubled every two years, for the 10 years between 1970 and 1980. This helped it to become a very large player very rapidly, at one time

---

[62]Ibid.

accounting for over 70 per cent of all synthetic fabric exports during that time.

It focussed on quality, so much so that a World Bank team which was visiting Indian mills in the early 1970s stated that Reliance was 'the only spinning mill that warranted the stamp of excellence based on developed country standards'.[63]

It was only when the company decided to integrate backwards into manufacturing the raw material, PFY, that Mukesh was called back from his MBA studies in Stanford to supervise the setting up of the plant in Patalganga, in Maharashtra.

Similarly, Mukesh has shown his expertise in having mastered this strategy very well. He had, at the time of first setting up Reliance Telecom, before the split between the brothers, laid down over 60,000 kms of optic fibre cable all over India. This was an unprecedented move which changed the connectivity in India at the time.[64] Reliance under Mukesh, then

---

[63]'Focus on Quality and the Desire for Control of Value Chain', AllFreePapers, accessed 6 November 2019, https://www.allfreepapers.com/Miscellaneous/Focus-on-Quality-and-the-Desire-for-Control/75181.html

[64]Krishna Gopalan and Rashmi K Pratap, 'Act II', *Outlook Business*, 30 March 2013, accessed 28 July 2019, https://www.outlookbusiness.com/the-big-story/lead-story/act-ii-1401

Flexibility and Integration of the Value Chain

in its second innings, sought to set up towers for its mobile telephony business. At the time, there were options to either set these up by oneself at a cost of ₹25 to ₹30 lakh or use someone else's tower on a monthly rental between ₹25,000 and ₹40,000.

But he came up with a third option, where he tied up with Indian Institute of Technology (IIT) Mumbai and developed a newer version of telecom towers costing less than ₹10 lakh, which were lighter, used less steel, were prefabricated, could be mounted on street lights and be operational within four days. A huge saving in costs and time, given that Mukesh had put in place the target of rolling out over 8,000 towers in Mumbai alone, a city where the combined population of all the four competitors' towers was about 3,600.[65] He is said to have invested around $36 billion on Jio's national 4G network and fibre optic infrastructure. This heavy level of capital expenditure had resulted in a few established players pulling back

---

[65] Aveek Datta, 'Mukesh Ambani seeks to future-proof RIL', *Fortune India* online, 7 July 2018, accessed 28 July 2019, https://www.fortuneindia.com/enterprise/mukesh-ambani-seeks-to-future-proof-ril/102103. (Note: corrected by the author to reflect the RIL balance sheet 2019 figures, originally quoted 74184 in the original article.)

their investments or even exiting the industry.[66]

LEARNINGS

This is an important and very significant lesson. RIL, under Dhirubhai, used the advantage of the favourable environment, to grow. The government policy had allowed exporters to import raw materials and machinery to set up industries for export. RIL used this to their advantage. The important factor here, is to see that they used this cycle very effectively, which not many people were able to do. To explain better, they exported the fabric which was of a very high quality and cost-effective (the costs must have been low due to their large capacity and efficient operations) and they got import benefits from the government. They used these import entitlements to import the latest machinery which additionally helped them get higher productivity, a better-quality product comparable to international standards. Hence, this becomes a self-fulfilling cycle, also what Jim Collins, an American author, has called

---

[66]ET Online, 'The Man with all the toys: Why Mukesh Ambani bought Hamleys', *The Economic Times*, 12 May 2019, accessed 29 July 2019, https://economictimes.indiatimes.com/industry/services/retail/the-man-with-all-the-toys-why-mukesh-ambani-bought-hamleys/articleshow/69264824.cms

Flexibility and Integration of the Value Chain

as a flywheel effect. The key learning here is to see that the effects of the actions that one takes help gain an advantage for the firm, which helps it get a higher advantage than the competitor. And because all these actions are aligned, the faster one drives this cycle, the bigger is the advantage that one gets.

Can you think of such advantages in your business?

This is probably what happened in the case of Reliance. It is true that the government export incentives did influence this step significantly, but only Reliance was able to use this to get a competitive advantage and it did it faster than the other players in the field.

Thus, the classic Reliance characteristics of speed, large capital expenses to save time to build world-class capacities and the focus on world-class quality and latest technology, helped it gain an advantage.

6

LOOK TO THE FUTURE FOR NEW OPPORTUNITIES: CHANGE THE STRATEGY TO FUTURE-PROOF THE COMPANY

Mukesh Ambani had the foresight to see the maturity come into the refining and petrochemical businesses and hence made a move into organized retail and telecom. Retail had been lagging since it had been introduced almost a decade ago, but it had picked up by 2019. Similarly, the telecom business had shown signs of increasing revenues. By 2019, Reliance Retail had over 10,000 stores and Reliance

Jio had over 300 million subscribers by mid-2019.[67]

RELIANCE RETAIL

Reliance Retail had 10,644 stores across 6,700 cities, with 100 million registered loyalty customers and had a footfall of 150 million in their stores for the year 2018–19.

Reliance Retail operates under the store brands of Reliance Fresh, Reliance Smart and Reliance Market stores. In consumer electronics, it operates under Reliance Digital, Reliance Digital Xpress Mini stores and Jio stores. In the fashion and lifestyle segment, it has Reliance Trends, Trends Women, Project Eve, Reliance Footprint, Reliance Jewels and AJIO.

There were press reports that Amazon was in discussions with Reliance to pick up a 26 per cent stake in Reliance Retail.[68] It was felt that due to

---

[67] Promit Mukherjee and Nidhi Verma, 'Reliance Industries sees telecom, retail driving growth', *Reuters* online, 18 April 2019, accessed 30 July 2019, https://in.reuters.com/article/reliance-results/reliance-industries-sees-telecom-retail-driving-growth-idINKCN1RU1J7

[68] Sanchita Dash, 'Here's why Jeff Bezos may want a stake in Mukesh Ambani'sReliance Retail', MSN.com, 1 August 2019, accessed 15 August 2019, https:// www.msn.com/en-in/money/news/heres-why-jeff-bezos-may-want-a-stakein-mukesh-ambanis-reliance-

the recent changes in the law, the deep discounting offered by the online retailers would soon go away and then the consumers would be looking at physical stores. This was a market that Amazon did not want to lose out on and hence their interest in finding a partner in India. There were also reports of Amazon being in discussions with Kishore Biyani-led Future group.[69]

Mukesh had foreseen that in retail, he wanted a fully integrated farm-to-fork strategy, with Reliance Retail handling the complete value chain. He has been steadily building up stores all over India and has been working on integrating the Jio customers into the backend provided by Reliance Retail, to possibly create a huge digital ecosystem combining retail and the mobile network.[70]

---

retail/ar-AAFajEi?li=AAgfW3S#page=2
[69]Ibid.
[70]TNN, 'Reliance retail juggernaut rolls out, aims to link farm to fork', *The Economic Times*, 4 November 2006, accessed 30 October 2019, https://economictimes.indiatimes.com/r-companies/reliance-retail/reliance-retail-juggernaut-rolls-out-aims-to-link-farm-to-fork/articleshow/312673.cms

JIO NETWORK

We are determined to connect everyone and everything, everywhere—always at the highest quality and the most affordable price.

—Mukesh Ambani at the Chairman's Speech at the Reliance AGM in 2018.

In 2018, the Institute for Competitiveness had forecast that Reliance Jio Infocomm Ltd. would be a key factor responsible for increasing India's per capita gross domestic product (GDP) by almost 5.65 per cent.[71]

At the 2018 Financial Times ArcelorMittal Boldness in Business Awards, where RIL was presented with the 'Drivers of Change' award, Mukesh shared how he conceived the idea of Jio. In 2011, his daughter, Isha, complained that the Internet connectivity was poor at her home, that too at the world's most expensive home.[72] 'Dad, the Internet in

---

[71] '12 things you probably didn't know about Mukesh Ambani', msn.com, 2 July 2019, accessed 9 August 2019, https://www.msn.com/en-in/money/photos/12-things-you-probably-didnt-know-about-mukesh-ambani/ss-BBQvk4r#image=6

[72] 'The incredible story of the billionaire who bought Beyonce for his daughter's wedding', msn.com, 9 January 2019, accessed 10 August 2019, https://www.msn.com/en-in/money/photos/the-incredible-

our house sucks.' As a result, the Yale graduate was unable to submit her coursework. This led Mukesh to the idea of Jio.

In his keynote address to FICCI Frames conference on the media and entertainment industry, in March 2016, Mukesh described his Jio venture as one of the largest transformational digital initiatives globally and also as the world's largest start-up, with an initial investment of ₹1.5 trillion.[73] This had been earlier pegged at ₹85,000 crore. This money has been used for investments in setting up telecom infrastructure, such as telecom towers, fibre-optic cables and purchase of spectrum and the revised amount could probably be the peak investment needed over the next three to four years.

At the event, Mukesh had stated that India was ranked 150 out of 230 countries worldwide for mobile Internet access. He said that as the world moves forward, it is our responsibility to digitally empower the 1.3 billion Indians and they should

---

story-of-the-billionaire-who-bought-beyonc%C3%A9-for-his-daughter%E2%80%99s-wedding/ss-BBRZDXV#image=21

[73]Vidhi Choudhary, 'Reliance Jio initial investment at ₹150,000 crore: Mukesh Ambani', Livemint, 31 March 2016, accessed 23 September 2019, https://www.livemint.com/Companies/ncT04NLRTtEMDEHAWdMPGN/Reliance-Jio-initial-investment-at-Rs150000-crore-Mukesh-A.html

not be left behind. He stated four key interventions that could be used to achieve a high growth rate in India, viz. coverage, quality, data and affordability. Coverage referred to the continuous mobile Internet connectivity regardless of where one is. India has currently only about 15 to 20 per cent coverage of high-speed mobile Internet, whereas the US had over 75 per cent of its population covered. Jio planned to start with 70 per cent coverage on day one and he hoped to achieve 90 per cent coverage by the end of 2017. Quality was measured as the speed and strength of mobile broadband. Jio proposed to offer speeds which were 40–80 times faster than the current prevailing speeds. The third factor was data capacity and quantity of data consumption per user. Jio's network was built to provide a capacity of over 10 GB per user, which was almost 100 times more than the 1.5 GB per user currently in India. The last factor was affordability and the service had to be affordable to every user in all parts of the country.[74]

Jio had been designed as an:

> Entire ecosystem which would allow Indians to live the digital life to the fullest. This ecosystem

---

[74]Ibid.

is made up of devices, broadband, powerful applications and services distributed to every doorstep in India. Jio's media offerings will include the most comprehensive library of programming of live and recorded music, sports, live and catch-up television, movies and events... Jio is about unleashing creativity and connected intelligence through the smartphone.[75]

Mukesh also described what he saw as major trends in the digital world—first being, the move towards video and images from the spoken word. A powerful video network would bring millions to a new platform and also have the power to change the way we learn, play, communicate and entertain.[76]

Secondly, he stated that digital technology is exponential and any exponential change would create opportunity. He explained that in the future, all the telecommunications, media and entertainment were converging to a telemedia world and the rules will change. The players will be different and not siloed like

---

[75]Vidhi Choudhary, 'Reliance Jio initial investment at ₹150,000 crore: Mukesh Ambani', Livemint, 31 March 2016, accessed 23 September 2019, https://www.livemint.com/Companies/ncT04NLRTtEMDEHAWdMPGN/Reliance-Jio-initial-investment-at-Rs150000-crore-Mukesh-A.html
[76]Ibid.

before. And the models will change from ownership to digital access.[77]

NEW COMMERCE ON THE MOBILE NETWORK

I am not building a telco, I'm building a digital platform company

–Mukesh Ambani, quoted by a Jio executive in
The Wall Street Journal.[78]

In August 2019, at the RIL AGM, Mukesh announced that RIL would launch Jio fibre commercially across India. This would be offering basic speeds, starting from a base speed of 100 Mbps and go up to 1 Gbps (compared to 90 Mbps, which is the average speed in the US). And these would be offered at prices which were one-fifth to one-tenth of the then-prevailing global rates. The cheapest data plan was ₹700 per month.[79]

---

[77]Ibid.

[78]Newley Purnell, 'Two Years Ago, India Lacked Fast, Cheap Internet—One Billionaire Changed All That', *The Wall Street Journal*, 5 September 2018, accessed 15 August 2019, https://www.wsj.com/articles/two-years-ago-india-lacked-fast-cheap-Internetone-billionaire-changed-all-that-1536159916?mod=e2tw

[79]ET Online, 'Mukesh Ambani unveils Jio Fiber & the mother of

Mukesh's vision of connecting kirana (grocery) stores across the country by providing the small businesses with tools to go online shows his inclusiveness of the small enterprises. Mukesh has worked out a means for small stores and businesses to build up and take advantage of the network and to grow their businesses, thereby overcoming any objections they may have against Jio. He has labelled this as new commerce, which he saw as a $700-billion business opportunity.[80]

Mukesh also announced a partnership between Microsoft and Jio, under which they would develop innovative cloud solutions, concentrating on the needs of Indian businesses. Thus, the partnership would have the benefit of Microsoft's Azure cloud platform, which is one of the three biggest players in the cloud hosting space (others being Amazon and Google).

---

all set top boxes', *The Economic Times*, 14 August 2019, accessed 15 August 2019, https://economictimes.indiatimes.com/tech/Internet/reliance-agm-mukesh-ambani-unveils-jio-fiber-the-mother-of-all-set-top-boxes/articleshow/70639869.cms?from=mdr
[80]Staff Writer, 'Jio GigaFiber launch, Saudi Aramco stake sale: Mukesh Ambani's key announcements at RIL AGM', Livemint, 12 August 2019, accessed 15 August 2019, https://www.livemint.com/companies/news/reliance-agm-2019-live-updates-mukesh-ambani-announces-launch-jio-phone-jio-gigafiber-1565586239462.html

Furthermore, Reliance also wanted to enter the Internet of Things (IoT) space. Jio's IoT venture was announced at the RIL AGM in August 2019, which would be a pan-India 4G network called Narrowband Internet of Things or NBIoT. It is estimated that this venture could deliver revenues of around ₹20,000 crore for the company.

Mukesh announced that all Jio fibre subscribers would get a landline phone connection free along with their subscriptions, given the fact that Jio had received more than 15 million registrations from nearly 1,600 towns across India. And the Jio set-top box would be able to accept cable TV signals from thousands of local cable operators who work with DEN, Hathway and GTPL.[81]

He also announced a new service, Jio First Day First Show to be launched in mid-2020.[82] Under this service, Jio subscribers would be able to see movies on their home broadband devices on the

---

[81]Ibid.

[82]ET Online, 'Mukesh Ambani unveils Jio Fiber & the mother of all set top boxes', *The Economic Times*, 14 August 2019, accessed 15 August 2019, https://economictimes.indiatimes.com/tech/Internet/reliance-agm-mukesh-ambani-unveils-jio-fiber-the-mother-of-all-set-top-boxes/articleshow/70639869.cms?from=mdr

same day they was released in the theatres.[83] This would severely affect the movie theatrical distribution business, disrupting it completely. The markets also seem to be concerned, with the share prices of the biggest theatrical exhibitors falling more than 8 per cent during trading hours.

Jio had also offered some services which it had bundled along with the phone subscription plans. It had offered JioTV, which offered more than 500 channels, JioCinema, which had a host of Indian films, JioMusic (now JioSaavn) having songs in 17 languages, JioMoney, a digital payments service and JioChat, a messaging app.[84]

Let us study the other impact of Jio.

The impact of high-speed data availability at very low costs has had a huge impact on Internet consumption and that of the businesses of other

---

[83]Bloomberg, 'View: Ambani cutting Reliance debt is bad omen for India's economy', *The Economic Times*, 14 August 2019, accessed 15 August 2019, https://economictimes.indiatimes.com/industry/energy/oil-gas/view-ambani-cutting-reliance-debt-is-bad-omen-for-indias-economy/articleshow/70669017.cms

[84]Newley Purnell, 'Two Years Ago, India Lacked Fast, Cheap Internet—One Billionaire Changed All That', *The Wall Street Journal*, 5 September 2018, accessed 15 August 2019, https://www.wsj.com/articles/two-years-ago-india-lacked-fast-cheap-Internetone-billionaire-changed-all-that-1536159916?mod=e2tw

Internet-related online giants. This has also been helped by the voice commands, icon-based swiping commands and voice search or voice messaging (in WhatsApp). This has opened up Internet access for a large number of people who have taken to Internet apps and who could not do so earlier, due to their inability to read or write. For WhatsApp, a messenger app owned by Facebook, India's 200 million users are its biggest market. In fact, users find it easier to use WhatsApp since one has to just sign up for the app by submitting their phone number. Hence, a large number of people who have never used email or Facebook can now use the service.

In the first year of its operations, it was stated that Jio transmitted more data than any other carrier in the world![85] In 2017, India's downloads of apps from the Google Play Store overtook those from the US.[86] And the monthly data traffic per user in India had jumped 570 per cent since Jio launched two years ago.[87] Jio had launched a low-cost phone on a returnable security deposit of $23, which enabled more users to use data services. This enabled more data usage.

---

[85]Ibid.
[86]Ibid.
[87]Ibid.

WHAT IS THE IMPACT OF JIO ON OTHER GLOBAL SOCIAL MEDIA GIANTS?

Facebook has admitted in its quarterly earnings calls that its quarterly growth was due to the presence of free data usage in India, mostly offered by Jio.

Amazon tweaked its business model to offer cash on delivery (COD) to cater to a new set of customers who did not have credit cards. Google launched a new version of its YouTube app, called YouTube Go, designed to work on inexpensive smartphones. It also created Tez, a mobile payment app for India that can work without a credit or debit card. Google is also working on making many of its services adaptable to work with local Indian languages.

On the other hand, Walmart has said that it was attracted by the large number of people going online, which served as an incentive to spend $16 billion to buy Flipkart, India's largest online retailer. Netflix, an online movie streaming site, is also one of the highest-grossing apps on the Google Play Store and Apple's App Store. It has now over half a million subscribers in India.[88] Undoubtedly, the presence of Jio's free data-streaming bandwidth has increased the usage of mobile apps.

---

[88]Ibid.

LEARNINGS

One can see Mukesh's vision to invest in the industries of tomorrow. The world was moving to cleaner fuels and renewable sources of energy, though Indian demand for oil was still strong. But Mukesh did not rest on his past successes and diversified into more consumer-facing businesses of retail and telecom. When he first started retail, he had the vision to go from 'farm-to-fork' to reduce the wastage in the food supply chain and use these efficiencies to reduce costs and offer good-quality products to Indian consumers.

The telecom business was built around providing low-cost Internet access to the users and then supplementing this with the telecom, entertainment around it. The retail would also plug in as an additional service to the Jio user-base.

This was an interesting proposition, as it shows the future as he had said, 'data is the new oil'. And clearly, Mukesh had tied up with the best to enter into this sector. He worked alongside the content creation for mobile, besides providing the network for mobile and Internet access. This way, he has created an entire ecosystem through which other players have also benefited. Thus, they too had a commercial interest in encouraging the growth of Jio which would grow as more users were attracted to the Jio network. Reliance customized applications for the Indian users on the Jio network, which would further enhance usage and attract more new customers.

Additionally, he has tied up with numerous start-ups that he had invested in, which would help Jio take the next step into IoT.

This is classic Mukesh strategy, as we discussed earlier, of entering into a new market with the best players in the field and using their technology to build up capacity very fast. World-class products and services at reasonable prices for the huge consumer markets is the proposition which is driving the new growth areas in RIL.

7
THE POWER OF TEAMS

Now, this is a lesser-known aspect of Mukesh Ambani's operations, but it was something that he had put into place, right from the time he was setting up his first plant in Patalganga. He had the foresight to bring in SOPs and SOCs, as has been mentioned in an earlier chapter. But what needs to be given due attention is that he has been successful in building up Reliance with excellent people who are driving the organization.

He has always sought out the best people and given them the freedom to operate. He has taken the talent from the public sector, and even expatriates when needed, to launch his new ventures. His Jio headquarters in Navi Mumbai, where Mukesh spends a couple of hours every Wednesday has been set up on the lines of an open office plan. The office does not have any hierarchy and functions as a flat organization.

This is a paradox, running contrary to Mukesh's usual practice of running the business in offices behind closed doors and under a strictly followed hierarchical structure in the refinery business. But this was done with the specific aim to attract and retain talent. Mukesh also believed that Jio was a start-up, and hence, it should behave as one. Hence the switch over to an open office plan.[89]

For example, his team at Jio is headed by expatriates, representing some of the most experienced people in the industry globally. In a newspaper article, it is said that over 15 per cent of the total 20,000 people working on Jio were expatriates working in key roles. These expatriates had been recruited from all over the world.[90]

---

[89]Sunny Sen, 'Mukesh Ambani's army of expats at Jio', *LiveMint*, 30 January 2018, accessed 11 September 2019, https://www.livemint.com/Industry/lHFD4WXCoWs4BPdiYgdFKJ/Mukesh-Ambanis-army-of-expats-at-Jio.html
[90]Ibid.

Some of the senior expatriates included former Deutsche Telekom executive Rainer Deutschmann, who was Jio's chief product and innovation officer. Ex-Sprint chief technology officer Mathew Oommen, an American with Indian roots, is the head of networks. Ex-Apple executive Stratos Davlos, a key person in the development of the Hello Jio voice assistant, is the head of platform and engineering. Technology development and automation are under Jordanian, Tareq Amin. Caroline Seifert was the chief brand and design officer but only for a year. Janina Anjuli Schmidt took over after Seifert as design lead. Then there is Shuming Li (from China), who overlooks all of Jio's Wi-Fi rollouts; Swedish data scientist, Nikola Sucevic leads data analytics development in areas of radio coverage and capacity, machine learning, and telecom data mining.

(A later news article,[91] mentioned that a few of these had left Jio, including Rainer Deutschmann (September 2017), Tareq Amin (May 2018), Ayush Sharma and Nikola Sucevic, assistant vice president and data science head (around May 2018).

---

[91]Danish Khan, 'Top Expats including Tareq Amin quit Reliance Jio', *ETTelecom*, 17 May 2018, last accessed 23 September 2019, https://telecom.economictimes.indiatimes.com/news/top-expats-including-tareq-amin-quit-reliance-jio/64206597

Persevere and Prevail Like Mukesh Ambani

This talent base was in part necessitated as Mukesh was building a network in India which had never been built anywhere in the world, an Long-term Evolution (LTE)-only network from scratch, which was 5G ready. This was a state-of-the-art technology, much more advanced than the 3G or 4G networks that the Indian players were using. This was at a time when local Indian players were still installing their 3G networks! Hence, Reliance had to pick up excellent talent from abroad, since this was a new venture for the first time in the world. Oommen is supposedly handpicked by Mukesh and had worked with Reliance Infocomm, Mukesh's earlier telecom company that had been handed over to brother Anil, post the family business split between them. Oommen is considered one of the top five people in the world in network technologies.[92]

The benefit of hiring top talent speaks for itself. The cost of servicing data and calls on the IP-based Jio network is only eight paise per minute as compared to 30 paise for the others, including a 14 paise interconnection usage charge.

---

[92]Sunny Sen, 'Mukesh Ambani's army of expats at Jio', *LiveMint*, 30 January 2018, accessed 11 September 2019, https://www.livemint.com/Industry/lHFD4WXCoWs4BPdiYgdFKJ/Mukesh-Ambanis-army-of-expats-at-Jio.html

The Jio office has been transformed keeping in mind these young expatriate hires. They now come to work in the Jio Navi Mumbai office dressed casually in t-shirts and jeans. Saturdays are now holidays and one of the canteens has even started serving non-vegetarian food on the campus. The employees also go in the evening to the gymnasium or to play tennis, often coming back to work wearing shorts![93]

His oil and gas operations are headed by PMS Prasad, a Reliance veteran, who has been in Reliance since 1981, and had worked under Dhirubhai. He had headed the team which had set up the Jamnagar refinery complex in 1999 and the gas discovery in 2002.[94]

---

[93]Ibid.

[94]'Meet the people who run Reliance Industries', *The Economic Times*, 23 January 2013, accessed 30 October 2019, https://economictimes.indiatimes.com/corporate-industry/meet-the-people-who-run-reliance-industries/the-core-team-pms-prasad-executive-director/slideshow/18162803.cms;

Anupama Airy, 'Ambani names key aide PMS Prasad for Reliance Jio's 4G telecom roll-out', *The Hindustan Times*, 27 February 2014, accessed 30 October 2019, https://www.hindustantimes.com/business/ambani-names-key-aide-pms-prasad-for-reliance-jio-s-4g-telecom-roll-out/story-UB9oUELdTphsQea5czfeYI.html

LEARNINGS

Mukesh Ambani has been smart to realize that he needs top-class professionals if Reliance is to grow. He has sought talent from all over the world and has not hesitated to hire across nationalities, borders and geographies to get the right person on the right job. He has family and friends in certain key positions, but these are also people who have proven themselves many times and are comparable to the best professionals anywhere. So Mukesh has ensured that Reliance is headed and operated by well-qualified and extremely competent professionals, and hence this could also be an influencing factor in the fast growth of Reliance. We are now seeing a consistent trend across all leading industrialists for hiring and empowering top-quality competent professionals.

This is a learning that most leaders, especially in family-run businesses, overlook. The emphasis is mostly on the self or family members, and hence professional teams are avoided. As has been seen in the success of most big businesses, their success has been attributed to the existence of good teams comprising of professionally qualified, experienced people. Mukesh realized this and set up his teams accordingly. He did not hesitate to bring in world-class foreign talent when he could not find local talent suited to the requirements of his ambitious projects.

8
REDUCE DEBT: BE RESPONSIVE TO THE ENVIRONMENT

In the Reliance AGM held in August 2019, Mukesh Ambani had made a series of announcements to reduce the debt in his company and to explain his clear direction for RIL to become a zero net debt company by March 2021. The company had invested ₹5.4 lakh crore in the previous five years on expanding and strengthening its oil to chemicals business, creating 4G wireless telecom network that offers high-speed Internet and in setting up India's largest retail chain. This had resulted in the total debt increasing to very

Reduce Debt

large amounts. This was a cause for concern at the RIL AGM in 2019, which Mukesh addressed in his speech.

RIL had earlier in 2019, formed two separate Infrastructure Investment Trusts (InvITs): Digital Fibre Infrastructure Trust and Tower Infrastructure Trust. The next step was for RIL to transfer Reliance Jio Infratel's fibre and the tower businesses into these trusts. The gross debt worth ₹1.07 lakh crore along with the assets were transferred to these trusts. RIL had got an investment of ₹25,215 crore in the Tower Infrastructure Trust, which had a 51 per cent stake in Reliance Jio Infratel. Mukesh had stated that their telecom infrastructure assets had been transferred to these two separate infrastructure trusts for consideration of ₹1.25 lakh crore, after which RIL ended 2018–2019 with a net debt of ₹154,478 crore.[95]

This may get a little number oriented, but I would request you to bear with me.

The second deal that RIL made was to get an investment of $15 billion for a 20 per cent stake sale to Saudi Aramco, approximately ₹1.1 lakh crore. This

---

[95]Nevin John, 'How does Mukesh Ambani plan to cut RIL debt to zero in 18 months?', *Business Today*, 13 August 2019, accessed 15 August 2019, https://www.businesstoday.in/top-story/how-does-mukesh-ambani-plan-to-cut-ril-debt-to-zero-in-18-months/story/372140.html

investment was in the RIL's oil-to-chemicals (O2C) division, which was hence valued at an enterprise value of $75 billion.

The above-mentioned partnership included all the RIL refining and petrochemical assets including RIL's 51 per cent in the RIL-BP petroleum retail joint venture.[96] This meant that the RIL-BP deal would finally have BP having 49 per cent, and RIL and Saudi Aramco holding 40 per cent and 10 per cent respectively. It was expected that RIL would get around ₹7,000 crore from the stake sale from BP.

This partnership would also provide 500,000 barrels of crude every day to RIL's Jamnagar refinery from Saudi Aramco on a long-term basis. (The total capacity of RIL's two refineries at Jamnagar was 1,800,000 barrels per day, so this was about 28 per cent of the total capacity)

These two agreements would help reduce the RIL debt to about ₹37,000 crore (₹1.54 lakh debts, less ₹1.1 lakh crore from Saudi Aramco and ₹7,000 crore from BP).[97]

Mukesh had also mentioned in the AGM speech, that RIL had received strong interests from strategic

---
[96]Ibid.
[97]Ibid.

Reduce Debt

and financial investors in their consumer businesses, namely, Reliance Retail and the telecom arm, Jio, which he expected to invest in the next few quarters, although the listing of these entities was not expected in the future five years.

Mukesh also stated that they were looking to sell some real estate assets and exit from some financial investments, thus increasing cash flow for repaying debt still further. Mukesh had stated that these steps would help reduce the debt to zero levels within the next two years since the investments had already been done and they needed only marginal investments for the future business growth needs.[98]

In October 2019, RIL announced that they would form a wholly-owned subsidiary under which all the digital initiatives and apps would be brought and RIL would infuse ₹1.08 lakh crore into this subsidiary. This subsidiary would also acquire RIL's equity investment of ₹65,000 crore in its telecom subsidiary Jio. This would make Jio a debt-free company and was said to be done to make Jio more attractive to strategic investors.[99]

---

[98]Ibid.

[99]'Reliance Industries share price hits fresh 52-week high on plan to form digital services platform company', *Business Today*, 29 October 2019, accessed 20 October 2019, https://www.businesstoday.in/

LEARNINGS

Mukesh has grown rapidly and RIL has seen phenomenal growth across three verticals: petrochemicals, oil and refining, and the other two new sectors, retail and Jio. This had been fuelled with borrowings which had an interest cost to pay. This raised the costs of operations. The volumes had grown, but the profits were still not achieved. (Projects like these are usually capital-intensive and take a longer time for the returns to come in.) Mukesh may have realized that the operations would be threatened if they did not reduce the debt that they had taken. Therefore, these steps may have been in that direction.

His ability to restructure company operations to attract investments from strategic investors is a smart move to help unlock the valuations for his shareholders.

Readers will remember that some other big companies had taken on debt, which they were unable to repay and hence their lenders had started bankruptcy

---

markets/company-stock/reliance-industries-share-price-52-week-high-plan-digital-business/story/387258.html;

Kalpana Pathak, 'Reliance Industries to form a digital subsidiary with ₹1 trillion, Jio to be net debt-free', Livemint.*com*, 25 October 2019, accessed 30 October 2019, https://www.livemint.com/industry/telecom/ril-to-form-a-digital-subsidiary-with-rs-1-trillion-jio-to-be-net-debt-free-11572020576946.html

Reduce Debt

proceedings against these companies. But Mukesh, by consciously choosing to reduce his company's debt to more manageable levels, demonstrates financial prudence. This is an attribute that leaders would be advised to learn from. Given the rising number of bankruptcy filings in India, this is a lesson that one should not ignore!

9
BUILD WORLD-SCALE CAPACITIES

Clearly, the family vision of dreaming big and executing big is evident here. The other advantage, as mentioned by Mukesh Ambani in his speech to the shareholders in 2018, stated that Reliance was operating much more than its installed capacity in the energy business. However, in the Jio business, they were operating at a capacity utilization of less than 20 per cent for a user base of 215 million customers. This showed that they had a huge potential for future growth without any additional capital expenditure.[100]

---

[100] Aveek Datta, 'Mukesh Ambani seeks to future-proof RIL', *Fortune*

He had stated that Reliance had invested about ₹2.5 lakh crore in creating an extensive digital network to offer a low-cost, high-speed mobile and broadband connection under Reliance Jio.[101]

Given the need for additional growth besides the oil and refining businesses, Reliance then focussed on retail and digital broadband under Jio. This could explain the investments in these sectors. His bets paid off when in June 2019, Reliance Retail and Jio contributed 32 per cent earnings before EBITDA of the consolidated total.[102]

However, according to Fortune India[103], the strategy in 2018 showed that Mukesh had moved the direction of his strategy from diversifying backwards, to integrating forward. This shows a clear intention to

---

India online, 7 July 2018, accessed 28 July 2019, https://www.fortuneindia.com/enterprise/mukesh-ambani-seeks-to-future-proof-ril/102103

[101] Ibid.

[102] Amritha Pillay, 'RIL has built foundation for next decade in FY19, says Mukesh Ambani', *Business Standard*, 21 July 2019, accessed 29 July 2019, https://www.business-standard.com/article/companies/ril-has-built-foundation-for-next-decade-in-fy19-says-mukesh-ambani-119072100035_1.html

[103] Aveek Datta, 'Mukesh Ambani seeks to future-proof RIL', *Fortune India* online, 7 July 2018, accessed 28 July 2019, https://www.fortuneindia.com/enterprise/mukesh-ambani-seeks-to-future-proof-ril/102103

differentiate and focus on creating value by offering higher-margin, newer businesses, rather than get economies of scale, as was being done earlier.

Hence, the energy sector would now move into niche chemicals, mobile telephony to be integrated into broadband and an overall digital platform to combine RIL's retail footprint to create a hybrid online-offline commerce platform.

Earlier, when RIL was investing in Jamnagar, it was at the first complex of its size in India, which was spread over 5,000 acres, and included, besides the refinery, plans for petrochemicals facilities, power generation plants, India's largest private port and the world's second-largest oil port. All this was built within three years!

LEARNINGS

Wealth is the product of man's capacity to think.

—Ayn Rand in *Atlas Shrugged*

RIL has been thinking against the grain and has come out right in front at most times. The example of the Jamnagar refinery is one example. As mentioned elsewhere in this book, the Jamnagar refinery was launched at a time when the normal returns on capital invested for refineries elsewhere were in the range of 6 to 8 per cent. The cost of capital at the time was 12 per cent. This would have meant a very high-risk venture, almost verging on foolishness, as it meant that the interest cost on the investment was more than the returns that one would be getting from it! An investment is supposed to make sense only when one can recover all the costs, including the cost of capital, which wasn't in this case.

But the Ambanis were undeterred by the prospects. They must have realized that they could not have reduced the cost of capital, so they worked on increasing the returns. They designed the refinery in such a manner that it was flexible enough to work with a range of raw materials, including the low-cost heavy crude, which not many refineries would buy. It also designed the plant to produce a host of goods based on the then-prevailing market prices, thus ensuring that they always had a higher margin on products being produced. This helped them get higher returns.

Mukesh believes in using the large scale as a competitive weapon, just like his father did. This was seen in their building of huge-scale facilities, often more than the total installed capacity in India, and sometimes over the forecasted future demand in India also! This was in line with the vision of catering to the global markets, rather than restricting to the domestic markets alone. They realized early on that they needed to be internationally competitive and to achieve this objective, they built 'best-in-the-world' competencies in spite of the then-prevailing high tariffs. They installed the largest facilities in the world in many product lines, including polyester. Reliance preferred to buy the best technology rather than compromise by buying partial solutions or cheaper technologies which were not as good—in line with what their competitors were buying. DuPont is a case in point, where Reliance offered $5 million, believing that it would be worth the money paid to get the opportunity to work with the best company in the field anywhere in the world.

Over time, Mukesh has shown the ability to handle situations which seem very difficult or even impossible. Reliance's strength is to figure out a way to overcome every hurdle, using solutions which seem very simple. There have been some sections of the press that have pointed out that the regulations seem to favour the Ambanis and this could also have been a contributor to their success. But as I mention later on, this advantage is something which many businessmen have been using. Secondly, the advantages are temporary, as any competitive advantage can be copied over time.

Build World-scale Capacities

So, there is an inherent pressure to be constantly competitive and always proactive in providing what the customer needs. And Reliance has been doing this consistently.

10
THINK BIG, DREAM BIG

On 18 January 2019, Mukesh Ambani announced that Reliance would consolidate and offer online shopping on Jio in partnership with Reliance Retail, on a new e-commerce platform which would compete with Amazon and Flipkart.

Now, he has shifted focus to a slightly higher end of the market, away from the low-cost high-volume market.

Reliance has taken steps to safeguard its future and ensure there is a steady path to growth by looking into the following areas announced in the 2019 AGM, 'Oil to chemicals integration, upgrading all fuels, recycling (plastic), integrating Jio and offline retail stores, venturing into gas marketing, transition to being a technology platform company'.[104]

As discussed earlier, backward integration has helped RIL get huge margins. It has also integrated forward by setting up its retail outlets (e.g. petrol pumps).

Mukesh has been following the strategy set by Dhirubhai's thought process, that Indian manufacturing could become world-class. As discussed earlier, he was amongst the first industrialists to build a plant which could be compared to the best in the world, both in terms of production volumes and output quality. 'My commitment is to produce at the cheapest price and the best quality', he insisted time and time again. 'Think big, think fast, think ahead', he would exhort colleagues.

Pre-Dhirubhai, most Indian plants were very small-sized, keeping in mind the limited vision of the promoters. 'The size of Reliance's facility represented a major departure from the "normal" Indian business practice of the time. Instead of creating a "safe" capacity based on a reasonable projection of demand,

---

[104]Aveek Datta, 'Mukesh Ambani seeks to future proof RIL', *Fortune India* online, 7 July 2018, accessed 28 July 2019, https://www.fortuneindia.com/enterprise/mukesh-ambani-seeks-to-future-proof-ril/102103

Ambani applied for world-scale capacity that could meet the cost and quality standards on a global basis,' says Sumantra Ghoshal, head of strategic planning at the London Business School and author of a major case study on Reliance.

JIO

As has been mentioned elsewhere in this book, Mukesh got the idea for the mobile and Internet from his daughter, who was complaining about her difficulty in submitting her coursework on the then-prevailing Internet speed.

At that time, even though there was a need to enhance the speed, there was doubt that consumers would pay for the service, given the fact that Indians were only paying about $2 per month on their cell phones and a large portion of this was for voice calls.

There were some rival companies at the time, which had started introducing 4G services in a few cities. But Mukesh did not compromise on his vision. He had different ideas.

Mukesh wanted to build a network which covered more than a few cities. He wanted to build a network which would cover over 18,000 cities and towns, and 200,000 villages, including reaching out to those places that did not even have electricity then! It was calculated that this effort would need more than 200,000 cell towers and over 150,000 miles of high-tech fibre-optic cables, which would be enough to circle the earth six times.[105]

LEARNINGS

Mukesh's vision of setting up large-scale, world-class plants is something that he has in common with Dhirubhai. The large-scale capacity leads to the lowest possible costs, much lower than those of his competitors. He matches this with innovative re-engineering of the business such that he can get higher profits from his business. An ability that he is able to replicate across whichever industry he has entered. Also, his pursuit of lower costs has not come at the cost of lowering quality, and this ability to offer world-class quality at reasonably low prices keeps them competitively ahead.

---

[105] Newley Purnell, 'Two Years Ago, India Lacked Fast, Cheap Internet—One Billionaire Changed All That', *The Wall Street Journal*, 5 September 2018, accessed 15 August 2019, https://www.wsj.com/articles/two-years-ago-india-lacked-fast-cheap-Internetone-billionaire-changed-all-that-1536159916?mod=e2tw

11
FOCUS ON WORLD-CLASS CAPACITIES, LOWEST COSTS: THE JAMNAGAR COMPLEX

Growth has no limit—keep revising your vision.

—Dhirubhai Ambani's mantra[106]

Growth is Life.

—Reliance vision on the company website.

---

[106]Ernesto J. Poza, 'Family Business', Reliance Industries (A), page 355, Case 14, Third Edition, Cengage Learning, 29 January 2009.

Focus on World-class Capacities, Lowest Costs

A story which has been stated in the media is about the time when the Jamnagar refinery was being built. During one of his visits to the Jamnagar refinery to check on its progress, Dhirubhai had taken a walk during the night to find that the work had ended for the day. He asked Mukesh why the work could not be done in three shifts. Mukesh contacted the contractors the next day and offered bonuses for meeting or exceeding the project deadlines. This simple step ensured that the Jamnagar complex was completed within 36 months at a cost which was 30 per cent to 50 per cent lower than comparable refineries in Asia. This was the first significant achievement, in a long list of many, which Mukesh did after joining the family business upon his return from Stanford.[107]

For those who may not know the full extent of the project, this was then the world's largest refinery, built for $6 billion, extending over 31 square kilometers. The infrastructure needed to support the refinery included a 350-megawatt power plant, two chemical plants, 105 miles of road, housing for 3,000 families, a seawater desalination plant and an information technology (IT) network to connect 50 servers and 2,500 terminals

---
[107]Ibid.

with 200 km of fibre-optic cables.[108]

THE JAMNAGAR REFINERY COMPLEX[109]

(Author's note: I would have normally not written about a project, but this is a story which has a lot of learnings, and hence I am including this here.)

BUILDING JAMNAGAR REFINERY NO. 2

As mentioned earlier in this book, the first Jamnagar refinery was built for $6 billion in 1999. The second refinery, which was built alongside the first, was an export-oriented unit and was designed to produce heavy crude and produce expensive types of fuel. The cost of the refinery was 40 per cent less than the international costs. It was built keeping in mind the mistakes made in the first refinery and at one-third the cost of building two huge refineries which were planned in Saudi Arabia.

---

[108]Ibid.
[109]ECN, 'Reliance Industries pushes to complete Jamnagar refinery', www.icis.com, 22 July 2007, accessed 9 August 2019, https://www.icis.com/explore/resources/news/2007/07/23/9046296/reliance-industries-pushes-to-complete-jamnagar-refinery/

THE SECRET?

The following methods were mentioned, for keeping costs under control, a lesson for any manager:

1. Compressing the implementation time. Reliance had done this by booking vendors' capacities well in advance and ordered all those items first, which had long lead times. This would help in getting their orders executed on time.
2. The equipment was standardized so that they could buy similar units in bulk, thus getting the benefit of larger volumes of a standardized product.
3. Reliance was also involved in every stage of the project and did not leave the contract execution only to the contractors.

THE SCALE?

I will quote verbatim from the website of ICIS, the world's largest petrochemical market information provider:

> Building the new refinery at Jamnagar involves over 200,000 engineering and supplier documents, the installation of 165,000 tonnes and 53m cubic

feet (1.5m cubic metres) of concrete, 138,000 tonnes of structural steel (equivalent to 15 Eiffel Towers), more than 4,400 pieces of major equipment in over a dozen complexes within the refinery, and 13m feet (4m metres) of piping. The project site covers an area larger than London, and more than 80,000 workers will be employed during the peak of construction—around the same number deployed in building the first refinery.[110]

The huge scale of the project compelled the lead contractor, Bechtel, to rework many of its processes to meet the deadlines in this extremely complex project. Bechtel had to set up a customized communication network to connect its engineers in London, Houston, Frederick, Toronto, Shanghai and New Delhi, virtually, so that they could exchange engineering drawings and time-sensitive data to meet the time schedules. They had ordered the equipment in advance in some cases, so that they could avoid getting stuck in the impending shortages that they foresaw. In some cases, they bought the equipment first and later designed around

---

[110] Accessed 7 November 2019, https://www.icis.com/explore/resources/news/2007/07/23/9046296/reliance-industries-pushes-to-complete-jamnagar-refinery/

what they had bought. Bechtel trained an army of RIL engineers at its facilities worldwide to help operate and maintain the refining complex.

Reliance had set up a facility in Jamnagar to train approximately 8,000 welders, 5,000 carpenters and 5,000 pipe fitters[111] to overcome any shortages of skilled labour. The project eventually involved 10 million hours of design work, four million cubic metres of concrete, 18,000 kilometres of electrical cabling, 15,000 kilometres of instrumentation cabling, 20,000 kilometres of piping and 250 kilometres of roads.[112]

When the project was completed in late 2009, it was regarded in the top 25 per cent highest globally ranked plants in capital efficiency and operating efficiency.[113]

As mentioned earlier, the Jamnagar refinery complex site has two refineries, the older one of 33 million tonnes per annum (tpa) and another export-

---

[111]ECN, 'Reliance Industries pushes to complete Jamnagar refinery', www.icis.com, 22 July 2007, accessed 9 August 2019, https://www.icis.com/explore/resources/news/2007/07/23/9046296/reliance-industries-pushes-to-complete-jamnagar-refinery/

[112]Kannan Ramaswamy, 'Reliance Industries: An Indian Family business comes of age in global energy and petrochemicals', Teaching Case TB 0303, Thunderbird School of Global Management, 2012. Page 2

[113]Ibid.

oriented unit of 35.2 million tpa[114]. In an article in July 2019, it was stated that as per the latest annual report of Reliance Industries, the complexity of the Jamnagar refinery had risen from 12.7 to 21.1.[115] This was helped by their commissioning of some additional expansion projects. (The first refinery was built with a Nelson Complexity Index [NCI] of 11.3 and the second one at 14).[116]

The complexity index (CI) is a measure of how low quality of crude oil can be processed by a refinery to produce the highest quality of refinery products like fuels and petrochemicals. The article stated that according to another report, the refinery had processed over 170 different types of crudes from 150 processed over the previous two years.

This was in comparison to other refineries. For

---

[114]PTI, 'Reliance's refinery complexity index rises to 21.1%', Moneycontrol.com, 26 July 2019, accessed 6 August 2019, https://www.moneycontrol.com/news/business/reliances-refinery-complexity-index-rises-to-21-1-4253171.html.

[115]PTI, 'Mukesh Ambani's RIL plans to only produce jet fuel, petrochemicals at Jamnagar refinery', *Business Today*, 12 August 2019

[116]ECN, 'Reliance Industries pushes to complete Jamnagar refinery', www.icis.com, 22 July 2007, accessed 9 August 2019, https://www.icis.com/explore/resources/news/2007/07/23/9046296/reliance-industries-pushes-to-complete-jamnagar-refinery/

example, the public sector government-owned Bharat Petroleum Corp Ltd's Bina refinery in Madhya Pradesh has a CI of near 10. The Hindustan Petroleum Corp. Ltd's (HPCL) refinery at Bhatinda has a CI of 12. And the Indian Oil Corporation Ltd (IOCL) refinery at Paradip, Odisha, has a CI of 12.2. Essar Oil's refinery was at 11.8.[117]

This has enabled the Jamnagar refinery to earn a premium of $4.3 a barrel over the Singapore Benchmark Margins.

WHAT IS THIS COMPLEXITY INDEX (CI)?

NCI is the measure by which the complexity of a refinery is measured. Any refinery above an NCI of 10 is considered a complex refinery. The complexity of the refinery refers to its ability to handle different types of crude, which is the raw material used, from which one gets the different petrochemical products like petrol, diesel and other products.[118] The crude quality ranges

---

[117] Kalpana Pathak, 'Why private sector cos score better on refining margins', *Business Standard*, 19 July 2019, accessed 6 August 2019, https://www.business-standard.com/article/companies/why-private-sector-cos-score-better-on-refining-margins-115071600173_1.html
[118] Ibid.

from heavy, high sulphur content, which is available at a low price to light, low sulphur content crude, which is more expensive and easier to process. One needs a high complexity refinery to process the lower-quality crude.

The basic business is to use the crude as the input and we get the petro products as the output, which are sold at market prices. Hence, having a refinery which has a higher complexity index allows one to buy cheaper heavier crude, which decreases your production costs. This, coupled with the fact that the Jamnagar refinery complex is amongst the world's largest refinery complexes in a single location, gives RIL huge cost savings.

The fact that RIL is pushing towards higher complexity and expanding at the same location shows their drive for higher efficiencies and lower costs, at world-class standards of production. This is one of the reasons why they have been consistently earning a premium over the comparable average industry margins.

The degree of engineering expertise that has gone into the Jamnagar facility can be estimated by a newspaper report which states:

In January 2018, RIL announced the successful commissioning of the world's first-ever Refinery Off-Gas Cracker (ROGC) complex of 1.5 million tonnes per annum capacity. The ROGC complex uses off-gases from Jamnagar refineries as feedstock, helping RIL emerge as one of the most efficient producers of polymers in the world. Petcoke gasification project, one of the largest clean initiatives in the world, uniquely turned Jamnagar refineries 'bottom-less' by converting low-value petroleum coke into syngas (synthesis gas). One of the most complex projects, it has integrated 83 process units with refineries and other downstream units operating in extreme conditions, with temperatures ranging from (-)190°C to (+)1,480°C, and pressure fluctuating from vacuum to 120 standard atmosphere.[119]

Reliance's refining complex, reported to be the largest in the world, has been designed in such a manner that it operates only on desalinated seawater. This ensures that the freshwater resources from lakes and rivers are

---

[119]PTI, 'Reliance's refinery complexity index rises to 21.1%', Moneycontrol.com, 26 July 2019, accessed 6 August 2019, https://www.moneycontrol.com/news/business/reliances-refinery-complexity-index-rises-to-21-1-4253171.html

hence made available for local communities to use.[120]

Another point worth stating is that the lessons of Patalganga were effectively used in the Jamnagar refinery. Therefore, while designing the Jamnagar refinery, integration of the input and the output was given extreme priority. This was needed, as the output could be either used as raw material to make another higher-priced product, or it could be used as fuel that could be utilized to generate heat in other parts of the process. This ensured that only 0.2 per cent of the output was wasted, which is commendable when compared to the global average of 5 per cent for refineries.[121]

The constant focus on efficiency led to Reliance being judged at the top in a Shell Benchmarking magazine in 2004, for the third consecutive year, in energy and loss performance amongst 50 refineries globally. This stated that Reliance was the world

---

[120]PTI, 'Reliance's refinery complexity index rises to 21.1%', *The Economic Times*, 26 July 2016, accessed 30 October 2019, https://economictimes.indiatimes.com/industry/energy/oil-gas/reliances-refinery-complexity-index-rises-to-21-1/articleshow/70397204.cms?from=mdr

[121]Kannan Ramaswamy, 'Reliance Industries: An Indian Family business comes of age in global energy and petrochemicals', Teaching Case TB 0303, Thunderbird School of Global Management, 2012. Page 2

leader in energy performance, and in operating costs, manpower costs and maintenance cost and plant utilization.[122]

Similarly, in the 41st AGM of Reliance, Mukesh announced that Reliance had more than doubled its network capacity in Jio, and even after adding 215 million customers to its network, its capacity utilization was less than 20 per cent. He added that they could multiply their subscribers without any additional investments! He also stated that the company was on its target to cover 99 per cent of the population with 4G LTE, which would give its network a wider coverage than any other network.[123]

LEARNINGS

It is a well-known fact and proven theory that most large-scale manufacturing operations, often result

---

[122]'Reliance Jamnagar refinery ranked best', *Business Standard*, 6 February 2019, accessed 11 August 2019, https://www.business-standard.com/article/economy-policy/reliance-jamnagar-refinery-ranked-best-104011301078_1.html

[123]ET Telecom, 'Reliance Jio doubles network capacity, can multiply users without additional investment', ETTelecom, 5 July 2019, accessed 23 September 2019, https://telecom.economictimes.indiatimes.com/news/reliance-jio-doubles-network-capacity-can-multiply-users-without-additional-investment/64866589

in lower costs due to economies of scale. Hence, most companies desire to increase their production capacities by pushing for higher sales volumes.

But Mukesh seems to have perfected this into an art. He has managed to squeeze profits by ensuring that his giant projects are built much before the deadlines, beating all previous records for commissioning projects, usually even faster than what his partners or vendors have built. His attention to the micro details including the scale-up of pipe-fitters and electricians for Reliance's Jamnagar plant, is exemplary and would probably be a case study for an ideal way to manage a project for the future!

12

DIVERSIFICATION INTO RETAIL: FOCUS ON BUYING ICONIC BRANDS TO CONSOLIDATE RETAIL PUSH

On 13 April 2019[124], a newspaper article reported that Reliance Retail was intending to lay a big bet on a digital wholesale marketplace for business-to-

---

[124] Rasul Bailay and Writankar Mukherjee, 'Reliance Retail has major plans in store for kiranas', 13 April 2019, accessed 23 September 2019, https://economictimes.indiatimes.com/industry/services/retail/reliance-retail-has-major-plans-in-store-for-kiranas/articleshow/68858751.cms?from=mdr

business (B2B) e-commerce. This was in line with the Chinese e-commerce giant, Alibaba. The marketplace would focus on products like smartphones, televisions, garments, spices and soap. The intended target audience was a range of retailers, including those located in remote villages.[125] The idea was to address the estimated 12 million kirana outlets that were majorly sourcing their products from traditional wholesale markets like Sadar Bazaar in Delhi or from distributors of large consumer companies. This platform would bring smaller kirana stores together with larger distributors and suppliers. The Reliance Retail platform would facilitate the servicing of even small orders through various modes. The buyers of these goods could choose to pick up these goods from the shops of their sellers or have them delivered at home on Reliance's network which was being created especially for this purpose. Reliance was also building the necessary infrastructure such as fulfilment centres for supplying fast-moving consumer goods (FMCGs), grocery and consumer electronics.[126]

In 2019, Reliance Retail got revenues of ₹130,566 crore, almost doubling the previous year's sales. They

---

[125]Ibid.
[126]Ibid.

added 2,829 stores during the year, of which 510 were added in the last quarter itself! By the end of the year, the retail arm had 10,415 stores with retail space of over 22 million square feet. Additionally, it operated over 8,000 Digital and Jio stores together by 31 March 2019.[127]

On 10 May 2019, it was reported that Reliance Brands Limited, owned by Mukesh Ambani, had signed an agreement to buy Hamleys, the world's oldest retailer, for an undisclosed sum. The agreement was signed with C Banner International, a Chinese company which had acquired Hamleys in 2015. Hamleys was founded in 1760 and had 167 stores across 18 countries, as in 2019. Hamleys's 88 stores across 29 cities in India were already being operated by Reliance Industries.[128] Darshan Mehta, CEO of Reliance Brands Limited, was quoted as saying, 'The worldwide acquisition of the iconic Hamleys brand.... is a long-cherished dream come true.'[129]

---

[127] https://www.jmfinancialservices.in/news/details/1083359, accessed 6 August 2019

[128] 'Hamleys: India's richest man Mukesh Ambani buys iconic toy store', BBC News online, 19 May 2019, accessed 28 July 2019, https://www.bbc.com/news/world-asia-india-48223903

[129] Ibid.

LEARNINGS

The passion and drive to attain a global scale is an underlying theme in Mukesh's thinking. For ages, under the licence raj and high interest and import tariffs, Indian industrialists were forced to think in terms of minimum-sized capacities. This led to suboptimal costs due to uneconomical plant sizes. But this was fine, as the limited and controlled production capacity in the country gave these industrialists almost monopolistic markets where they could price high and make obscene profits. But, as we have seen, the entry of Reliance with plant capacities which were more than the total demand in India has changed the game completely and forever.

Dhirubhai, and later Mukesh, played on the basis of new rules, where capital was not a constraint and the import tariffs were reduced on the basis of export earnings/commitments. And then suddenly, the world was their market, with the domestic market getting a benefit of the large capacities. The other local competitors caught on, but by then Reliance was far ahead. Since then, the most economical, largest possible capacity is the determinant factor in deciding plant sizes, based on global markets. The overall capacity in the industry becomes seemingly irrelevant.

Diversification into Retail

Reliance leaves the competition far behind, as it drives unheard-of efficiencies by doing things differently. By the time the competitors figure out what they have done, Reliance has already moved on to their next step.

There could not be a better case for the strategist to learn from. Like them or hate them, but you cannot ignore the fact that Reliance has redefined every industry that they have touched, with large-scale volumes, audacious goals and a more efficient way of doing things which confounds their biggest critics. And the way that Reliance has managed to get higher margins just illustrates that one can extract higher margins, if one is innovative. The story of how Mukesh and Reliance have succeeded in extracting extra profit margins in industries such as refining, where even the best experts had taken the below-interest-costs margins as standard is a very valuable lesson to all leaders. Do not take the industry experts opinion as a given. Question everything and work out better ways to make businesses better.

I am not going into favourable regulatory or political environments since these are variable and can change into adverse situations quickly. But what is noteworthy is that the sustainability of Reliance is coming from their ability to think differently in every industry that they enter into and make money in different aspects of the industry, which had always been there, but were ignored by their competitors.

The functioning of most start-ups is based on opportunities which may have been overlooked by the existing players, and they work on that. The laws may not be clear at the moment, so they may function on the edge of the law. For example, Uber, Airbnb, WeWork, etc. are some start-ups which have been facing various regulatory controversies while regulators grapple with the legality of their operations. So, from a different viewpoint, a student of management should probably learn how Reliance under Mukesh is functioning like a start-up. Looking for fresh ways to be profitable, pursuing a huge scale and at the same time being hyper-efficient with quality and innovation, looking to exploit opportunities that oftentimes the others may have missed.

In retail, Mukesh did not just enter into pure-play retail. What he did was to increase his margins to tie up with foreign brands wanting to come into India, and then jointly set up stores in India, thus getting a wider portfolio of brands to offer and getting huge opportunities to learn about the tastes and preferences of Indian consumers. This way, you make higher margins than by just selling commodity products.

13

EYE ON THE FUTURE: ALWAYS HUNTING FOR VALUE ADDITION

Mukesh Ambani had indicated by his purchases that he intended to make a dent in the e-commerce sector. He had made a series of purchases, either of companies or of stakes in various companies, which was probably intended to help face the existing e-commerce giants, including Amazon and Walmart/Flipkart.[130]

---

[130]Bloomberg, 'A look at Mukesh Ambani's US$2.5 billion shopping spree provides an insight into how he plans to take on Amazon in India', 8 April 2019, accessed 23 September 2019, https://www.scmp.

Mukesh is not happy resting on his laurels. He has set his sights on the e-commerce sector and has been acquiring companies. He acquired an 87.6 per cent stake in Fynd for ₹295 crore in 2019. Fynd is an e-commerce technology platform which provides solutions to merchants to manage their sales and inventory across multiple demand channels. Fynd was one of the first start-ups to get into the online to offline (O2O) space and is supposedly said to be a part of Reliance's intention to compete with international retail giants such as Amazon and Walmart. This could also be seen as Reliance's move into e-commerce, after the rollout of Reliance retail stores. This move shows that RIL has shifted its focus to technology-driven digital and e-commerce initiatives, from its traditional businesses of oil, gas, petrochemicals and refining.[131] A Bloomberg intelligence analyst had stated that the deal size of the acquisitions may seem small, but they could be seen as a move towards assembling a team of talented people who could, later on, be used for

---

com/business/companies/article/3005203/look-mukesh-amabanis-us25-billion-shopping-spree-provides

[131] Srishti Deoras, 'With its start-up acquisition spree, Reliance might soon be a Tech Powerhouse', 7 August 2019, accessed 20 August 2019, https://www.analyticsindiamag.com/with-its-startup-acquisition-spree-reliance-might-soon-be-a-tech-powerhouse/

building bigger projects.[132]

Since 2017, RIL has invested in over 20 start-ups. To get an idea of the acquisitions, let us look at 11 companies in which RIL has invested.

1. **Haptik:** One of the world's largest conversational Artificial Intelligence (AI) platforms which could be used to provide users with conversational AI-enabled devices capable of conversing in multiple languages. In other words, this provides customer support chat services using AI. The cost of acquisition was ₹700 crore.
2. **Grab A Grub** will help Reliance initiatives to deliver food, groceries and other merchandise using bikes as a delivery mechanism in a hyperlocal method.
3. **Infibeam Avenues** will contribute to the creation of e-commerce marketplaces.
4. **Saavn:** A music streaming platform powering Amazon Alexa in India.

---

[132]Bloomberg, 'A look at Mukesh Ambani's US$2.5 billion shopping spree provides an insight into how he plans to take on Amazon in India,' 8 April 2019, accessed 23 September 2019, https://www.scmp.com/business/companies/article/3005203/look-mukesh-amabanis-us25-billion-shopping-spree-provides

5. **Radisys:** To enhance Jio's presence in 5G, IoT and open-source architecture adoption.
6. **Reverie Language Technologies:** A Bengaluru-based local language technology service start-up, its cloud-based, language as a service (LaaS) platform is expected to help RIL extend its reach into various Indian markets, as this technology will help them deliver their applications and content in local languages in real-time.
7. **Embibe:** An online education platform, of which Reliance acquired a 72.69 per cent stake in April 2018.
8. **EasyGov:** A data solutions and software company.
9. **SankhyaSutra Labs Private Limited:** A high-performance computing software simulation services company.
10. **NetraDyne Inc:** A US-based AI start-up that focusses on driver and fleet safety using AI.
11. **Vakt Holdings:** A blockchain technology company which will help Reliance build a digital ecosystem using the technology.

In July 2018, Mukesh outlined in his shareholders' address his plan to get a share of the growing online shopping sector, which was estimated by Morgan Stanley to grow in size to $200 million from $30 million in 2018. Additionally, it was estimated by Cisco Systems Inc, that India's smartphone users would grow to 829 million by 2022 from a projected 500 million in 2019. This growth in smartphone users was expected to provide an exponential increase in the demand for online services and products ranging from music, food delivery, electronic gadgets and apparel. Mukesh plans to involve Reliance Retail and Jio here. The platform is expected to use augmented reality, holographs and virtual reality to create an immersive shopping experience, and was expected to contribute just as much as the refinery and other main businesses of Reliance by 2028.[133] This step was also supposed to include the mom-and-pop (kirana) stores, which made up a large chunk of the Indian retail market.

These acquisitions are adding brands, technology and expertise to Reliance's repertoire without adding

---

[133]Bloomberg, 'A look at Mukesh Ambani's US$2.5 billion shopping spree provides an insight into how he plans to take on Amazon in India', *South China Morning Post*, 8 April 2019, accessed 23 September 2019, https://www.scmp.com/business/companies/article/3005203/look-mukesh-amabanis-us25-billion-shopping-spree-provides

significantly to its debt.[134] But coupled with the telecom network, the Reliance ecosystem was built well to exploit advantages for the digital economy especially in areas such as music, entertainment, education and financial services.

LEARNINGS

As seen in the earlier chapter on the retail industry, Mukesh would like to move away from the commodity sales to sales from higher value-addition products. One needs to figure out what the customer needs and how to provide it cost-effectively. Also, Mukesh has been working on not just setting up a mobile network at a very high fixed cost, but he is seeking to consider how he could enhance usage for his customers while using the network. He is investing in all those external activities which would attract a user to continue using the Jio network and in return Reliance could make profits. So, the typical industries would be music, movies, shopping, social media, etc. And if Reliance can set up these features in-house, then they stand to have greater engagement with their customers and more options for business.

---

[134]Ibid.

Let us try to understand the economics of the digital space using a very simple example. Readers will have to appreciate that the economics of the digital space is a little different. For example, if a tailor was making a shirt by hand, then he would incur the costs every time he makes one. In case of, for example, an automated robotic factory making the same shirt, the cost of the factory would have already been incurred at the very beginning (also called as sunk costs, since the costs are sunk into the machinery and are assumed as not recoverable). In such a case, the cost of an additional shirt would be lower, since only the additional cost of say, the materials and electricity to make that additional one shirt would be incurred (also called variable costs, since the costs vary with the final output produced). So, in the case of a refinery, the cost is incurred upfront (I need to buy and commission the full refinery before I can get the first barrel of the finished product). So, the first barrel of oil is the most expensive, as I have to spend the entire capital cost to get it. Thereafter, the second barrel of oil will cost me only the variable costs for that barrel of oil which is very little compared to the cost of the refinery.

Therefore, the only way to make money in this model is to do one of the following: reduce the costs of the raw materials, reduce the cost of operations or increase the selling price of the finished products being offered.

Mukesh has been working on all three. In the refining business, the end price is fixed by the external factors, such as geopolitical conditions, demand and supply, etc., which are normally outside the control of any one company. Reliance has made its operations efficient, by having the largest refinery in the world, so it can get the benefits of lowest costs as compared to its competitors who have relatively smaller capacities. It has ensured that it can buy lower-cost raw material due to its higher CI (explained in the earlier chapter). And for the end products, it is working on making not one product, but a range of products so that it produces what could offer it the highest margins.

Similarly, in the digital space, the cost of making a digital movie is a one-time cost. Once you have a digital copy, then all the costs are incurred on making that first copy. Then, for every additional copy, one does not have to incur any variable costs, and these are zero. For example, I can make more digital copies and give it to unlimited customers, at no additional costs.

Now, what Reliance Jio has done, is install a digital path into a customer's home (Jio Fiber) or handsets (Jio Mobile network). With this, it can offer music, movies, online shopping, etc. as extra services.

The cost of the network has already been incurred. Every additional service it can offer allows Reliance an opportunity to make money by offering these services. This is a platform or ecosystem strategy, which Apple, Amazon and Google have been trying to do for quite some time now. The idea is to make the customer so dependent on one company that it does not go to any other competing company. Then this company can offer an increasing range of services from which it derives a constant revenue stream.

The most significant factor is that most of these companies offer these services free in return for customer information, which the customers give voluntarily. (For example, Google offers free email on Gmail or free search.) Customers are not bound and are free to move to competition, but the original company's products and services are so good that most customers do not want to shift out.

This way, Reliance Jio is seeking to offer its customers a whole bouquet of services, besides 'plain vanilla' Internet and communication services. Its ability to make profits will depend on how unique and reliable its services are, as compared to the competition. So, the digital space will be different, from the physical products space, as the competitors are not bound by physical geographical boundaries. For example, start-ups could, in the short term, need not set up physical facilities in India initially and could serve customers in India based out of the US. They could seek to establish a physical presence only once the local business justifies the need.

The digital space will be a new space for Reliance to operate in, and it has understood this well. Hence the move to acquire more companies for their talent and technology which can be used to serve their customers better.

These help companies to break out of the commodity price wars. The fact that they can do this in the oil and petrochemical space and also mobile and retail space, is a lesson for leaders, that one can differentiate in any industry; one just needs to think differently.

14
CHANGE BUSINESS MODEL TO BE RELEVANT: OIL-TO-CHEMICALS (O2C) STRATEGY

Reliance has developed a future-ready Oil-to-Chemical strategic vision to progressively, transform the Jamnagar refinery from a leading producer of fuels to chemicals

—Reliance Annual Report 2018–19

In 2019, Mukesh Ambani announced plans to reduce their revenues from fuels and produce only jet fuels and petrochemicals at the Reliance Jamnagar refinery.

The refinery was at that time, sourcing crude from all over the world, and then converting it into petrol, diesel, liquefied petroleum gas (LPG), jet fuel, naphtha and other value-added fuels. Some of these products are further used in the production of petrochemicals which is used for making plastics and other products.

The idea was to change the product mix and use this crude to convert only to jet fuel (or aviation turbine fuel [ATF]) used by aircraft and other high-value products. This will ensure that the refinery is ready for the future environment where the sale of petrol and diesel-driven cars is expected to decline and electric vehicles are expected to take off. This will also lead to a reduction in the demand for products such as petrol and diesel.

They are also making investments in plants to support this move towards higher-value chemicals. A newspaper report stated that Reliance intended to become debt-free by March 2021,[135] by repaying its debt which stood at ₹1.54 trillion at the time (September 2019). The article also stated that the

---

[135]Kalpana Pathak and Pallavi Pengonda, 'Reliance Industries likely to go on a spending spree after becoming debt-free', Livemint, 23 September 2019, accessed 25 September 2019, https://www.livemint.com/companies/news/ril-likely-to-go-on-a-spending-spree-after-becoming-debt-free-1569261078670html

company may then start investing heavily to move its chemical business up another notch. This move was a part of the Reliance O2C strategy to transform the Jamnagar refinery from a primarily fuel producer to a higher-margin chemical manufacturer. Reliance has developed a multi-zone catalytic cracking process that converts a wide range of feedstock to high-value propylene and ethylene. The company's plans include reduction of all refined products that are priced lower than crude. It plans to manufacture chemicals at the initial stage. Subsequently, it would plan to cease petrol and diesel as a part of the plan to move into electric mobility as transport fuel demand declines.[136]

Another analyst observed that the company has provided a phase-wise road map of over 70 per cent conversion of crude to high-value petrochemicals over 10 years. New complexes in Asia and the Middle East are announcing projects with 25 to 40 per cent crude to chemical conversion.[137] Reliance's announcement would mean that the petrochemical capacity would

---

[136]Ibid.

[137]PTI, 'How Mukesh Ambani-led world's biggest refinery is bracing for an EV future', *Business Standard*, 11 August 2019, accessed 26 September 2019, https://www.business-standard.com/article/pti-stories/reliance-to-produce-only-jet-fuel-petrochemicals-at-jamnagar-after-oil-to-chemical-strategy-119081100152_1.html

have to be increased and at current capex levels of $800 million per tonne, the capital expenditure was estimated to be ₹1,120 billion.[138] It built the world's first-ever Refinery Off-Gas Cracker (ROGC) complex of 1.5 million tonnes per annum and is importing ethane from the US to produce petrochemicals. Reliance has also started petroleum coke (petcoke) gasification projects which will convert the Jamnagar refinery complex into a 'bottomless refinery' by the conversion of refinery residue into synthetic gas.[139]

This is how, gradually, Reliance seeks to preserve and upgrade current refinery margins along with maximizing asset utilization for sustainable competitive advantage in chemical costs. The intention of Reliance to be a major player in the chemicals space shows that Mukesh will not hesitate to start another major spending spree, immediately after a seven-

---

[138] Kalpana Pathak and Pallavi Pengonda, 'Reliance Industries likely to go on a spending spree after becoming debt-free', Livemint, 23 September 2019, accessed 25 September 2019,
https://www.livemint.com/companies/news/ril-likely-to-go-on-a-spending-spree-after-becoming-debt-free-1569261078670.html

[139] PTI, 'How Mukesh Ambani-led world's biggest refinery is bracing for an EV future', *Business Standard*, 11 August 2019, accessed 26 September 2019, https://www.business-standard.com/article/pti-stories/reliance-to-produce-only-jet-fuel-petrochemicals-at-jamnagar-after-oil-to-chemical-strategy-119081100152_1.html

year investment cycle that resulted in the leadership position that Jio has currently managed in the Indian telecom space, disrupting all the current players. This move helps Reliance maintain its margins. It also shows that the company has adapted to future trends and has modified its operations to be able to operate more effectively in tomorrow's markets.

> The fundamentals of the Jamnagar oil-to-chemicals strategy are to employ advanced molecule management to upgrade the refinery intermediate streams, by value.
>
> The Jamnagar oil-to-chemicals objectives are to preserve as well as upgrade existing refinery margins, while maximizing asset utilization, for a sustainable competitive cost of chemicals. RIL has developed a disruptive technology innovation, a Multizone Catalytic Cracking (MCC) process, which converts a wide range of feedstock to high-value propylene and ethylene in a single riser. This technology, protected by Reliance's IP, shall underpin Jamnagar's oil-to-chemicals mission.
>
> The oil-to-chemicals programme is a roadmap implemented over a long-time horizon, based on market outlook and price triggers for refinery fuel products. The ultimate goal is to achieve greater

than 70 per cent conversion of crude refined in Jamnagar, to competitive chemical building blocks of olefins and aromatics.

—Reliance Annual Report 2018–19, Page 59

The report also stated that the Jamnagar refinery would eventually be producing jet fuels and petrochemicals, once its migration to the O2C was done. The plans were also to stop producing any refined products, whose prices were lower than the crude prices. These would be converted to chemicals. This step was taken as protection to stop producing petrol and diesel, given the declining demand for transportation fuels in favour of electric vehicles globally.

Another newspaper article mentioned that the stakeholder sale to Aramco, the Saudi oil giant, could signal that Ambani no longer sees hydrocarbons as the future and that the days of Big Oil as a cash generator could be numbered.[140] Mukesh has been attributed with a keen business sense and a good sense of timing for his business decisions.

---

[140]Sundeep Khanna, 'Opinion: A deal that shows the end of an oil-and-gas-super-cycle', *LiveMint*, 14 August 2019, accessed 23 September 2019, https://www.livemint.com/opinion/columns/opinion-a-deal-that-shows-the-end-of-an-oil-and-gas-super-cycle-1565802761097.html

Change Business Model to Be Relevant

For example, one can just look at the oil price super-cycles which began in 1861, and the third and final one which began around 1996. This was fueled by the rapid growth in China and other emerging markets, which in turn increased the demand for oil and other commodities. This cycle is now showing signs of slowing down following the slowdown in these markets.

On the other hand, Reliance, under Mukesh, took advantage of this growing phase of the oil super-cycle. It commissioned the world's largest greenfield refinery in 2000, having invested $6 billion at a time when the oil prices were just beginning to rise. Crude oil prices rose rapidly from the average low prices of $12.28 per barrel in 1998, to $109.45 per barrel by 2014 (thus rising to new highs over 15 years), to a peak of $144 in mid-2008. These high prices resulted in huge profits for Reliance, due to their foresight in having invested earlier in this sector.[141]

However, oil prices have now begun to drop to much lower levels and are not expected to increase again. World Bank has forecast that these prices would be around $70 per barrel in 2030. This would be due to the discovery and usage of other alternative

---

[141] Ibid.

sources of energy to meet the growing energy needs, which would make additional fresh investments in traditional sources such as coal, gas and petroleum look unattractive.[142]

Furthermore, there is the challenge of declining automotive sales over the last two years, which has further caused the reduction in fuel demand. Auto vehicle fuels account for more than half of the total oil-product demand.[143]

With the increase in the number of electric vehicles and the rise in demand of alternative fuels such as LNG and hydrogen, it causes a risk to the demand for fuels like diesel and petrol. This is expected to have an increasing impact on the fuel demand in the next five years, with the decreasing trend already apparent in certain geographies and market segments. This will result in refiners reducing their outputs. Oil refining has the lowest margins in the oil industry value chain.

Aramco, on the other hand, is one of the world's largest oil producers. It was to announce its initial public offering (IPO), stated to be the world's largest, at about $2 trillion. It was postponed due to the four drone strikes in September 2019, which affected its

---

[142] Ibid.
[143] Ibid.

ability to deliver and reduced its output by 50 per cent.

Aramco needs to have downstream assets in oil, gas and petrochemicals to ensure its continued profitability. It has a huge cash pile which may help it hedge its bets. Aramco faces the dual threats of decreasing demand from more environment-conscious customers who are fast moving to other alternatives and the disruptive innovators who are working on making their basic product obsolete. Hence the need for Aramco to buy additional assets to integrate its operations and hope to preserve margins in an otherwise seemingly mature market by having synergies between the world's largest producer and the world's largest integrated refinery and petrochemicals complex.[144]

With Mukesh choosing to sell off a 20 per cent stake to Aramco, valuing his business at $75 billion, in what is termed as the biggest foreign investment in the history of Reliance; he has chosen to plan his attention on other more profitable markets while using the funds received, to reduce his debt. There is a structural change in the industry and Mukesh has

---

[144] Reuters, 'Reliance to sell 20% stake in oil-to-chemicals business to Saudi Aramco: Mukesh Ambani', *Business Today*, 12 August 2019, accessed 23 September 2019, https://www.businesstoday.in/current/corporate/reliance-to-sell-20-stake-in-oil-to-chemicals-business-to-saudi-aramco--mukesh-ambani/story/371998.html

once again shown great insight and an uncanny ability to ride this wave, right in the front, before anyone else.

LEARNINGS

Flexibility to change the business model to ensure that one is in line with the current trends also ensures that the business does not get disrupted or loses its customers. Based on these scenarios, we find that Mukesh has been working on making his petroleum and oil business more efficient, and at the same time, he has an eye on future environmental changes.

Leaders have to constantly consider three scenarios: what their past was, what their present is and what their future is going to be. (This is similar to Vijay Govindarajan's Three Box Model or McKinsey's Three Horizons Model.)

They have to keep an eye on what their legacy has been, and how they have arrived at the current state. Sometimes, entrepreneurs pay a lot of emphasis on one aspect alone, and live in yesterday's world, still imagining the scale of grandeur of the earlier businesses. They fail to accept the current reality and live in denial. These businesses may have been leaders in the past but cannot survive the harsh realities of the current-day scenario. We saw many licence raj legacy businesses go this way and perish. This also happens when the markets suddenly change and only the most nimble have the chance to react to the change. This is also seen in family businesses where the older generation is still running the show in the fashion that made them successful in the past, refusing to change their ways, as they knew that was the way they had been successful and they are of the mistaken belief that carrying on the same way, will keep them profitable. This method refuses to acknowledge the change in the environments.

The second task that has to be done is to keep the present business sustainable and profitable. They have to preserve their cash flow by keeping these cash engines going and ensuring that they have money to survive and grow. Most entrepreneurs usually do this part well, but they are too busy being operationally efficient to worry about the future. Additionally, the risk is that if one does not invest in the business but just keeps on milking it, there could come a time when the business is unable to sustain even with the existing level of profits.

Then there is the third part, which is to keep an eye on the future and try to estimate where the industry and the business are going and to make mid-course corrections to ensure that one lands up there. This is perhaps the most important aspect of the leader; to ensure that the business will sustain and be relevant to its customers even in the future.

Mukesh has seen two trends which he has started to work on within his company: one is the need to cut down debt in an increasingly risky world and the second is the shift away from oil towards electric and other renewable sources of energy, thus compelling an urgent need to find another business model to keep Reliance going and to utilize their investments better. The move to chemicals, and the new growth businesses, mobile and retail is perhaps in line with this philosophy. How these play out is something we shall see only in the future, but the fact remains that Mukesh has taken steps to keep his company relevant and in the position it has traditionally been in, that is, right at the top of any list.

15

CREATING OPPORTUNITIES: THE GREEN BELT AT JAMNAGAR

What may be a lesser-known fact is that the world's largest refining complex also has another feather in its cap. It is also the site of Asia's largest mango orchard, putting Reliance on the path to becoming India's largest mango exporter.[145]

---

[145] Kumar Amitav Chaliha, 'Reliance Industries pushes to complete Jamnagar refinery', *ICIS online*, 22 July 2007, accessed 23 September 2019, https://www.icis.com/explore/resources/news/2007/07/23/9046296/reliance-industries-pushes-to-complete-jamnagar-refinery/

Persevere and Prevail Like Mukesh Ambani

How this came to be is an interesting story in itself.

Every refinery is required by law to maintain a green belt around the plant. This is done to neutralize any pollutants arising from the refinery. This green belt usually has trees grown in it as per the regulatory requirements. I have seen some steel plants where the management has shown me several flowering and non-flowering trees around the plant; a pretty routine affair, done just to comply with the laws of the land.

But Reliance had to do this differently! In the typical Reliance way, this was also done on a large scale, with a 7,500-acre green belt around the refinery. And yes, it was green. The only difference was that the trees grown here were not flowering or non-flowering.

This green belt is home to over 100,000 mango trees producing 110 varieties of mangoes. The green belt also grows other products such as guavas, pomegranates, oranges and cashews. A unique aspect of all the trees in this orchard is that they are not allowed to grow over 10 feet, so that it becomes easier to maintain and pluck the fruit.[146] Reliance has invested a competent team to ensure that the orchard has high productivity.

The orchard grows Indian mango varieties such

---

[146] Ibid.

as Kesar, Alphonso, Ratna, Sindhu, Neelam and Amrapali, along with foreign species such as Tommy Atkins and Kent from Florida, and Lily, Keitt and Maya from Israel. The orchard is irrigated by wastewater and desalinated water from the refinery. More than half the output from the orchard is exported, and the balance is sold nationwide through the Reliance Fresh grocery chain, a part of the Reliance Retail network. A Reliance spokesperson has said that the margins on the mangoes were higher than any other petroleum products manufactured by Reliance![147]

Similarly, on a visit to the Jamnagar plant somewhere around 2013, I was surprised to find out that the Reliance Jamnagar refinery was desalinating seawater and not using any water from the public sources! It was using seawater and desalinating it. A desalination plant removes the salt from seawater, but it is a very high energy-intensive process. And where did the energy come from? From the heat generated in some of the refining processes! So effectively, Reliance was using free energy (which would otherwise have been wasted, if not used elsewhere). And the treated wastewater is used for irrigating the trees in the green belt.

---

[147]Ibid.

LEARNINGS

This is a small incident and may not be deserving of a full chapter, but this brings out a very important point, which I think is a great learning for entrepreneurs: using limitations to create profits.

By definition, entrepreneurs have a shortage of resources and hence, frugality becomes a necessity. One has to be innovative and resort to 'jugaad' to find solutions.

The learning in this case, is the fact that Reliance has used resources which would otherwise have been wasted, productively. This attitude of looking at things from a different angle is what separates the winners from losers. We need to have the ability to look at adversities in such a manner and consider how we can exploit these to our advantage. We will find that unless we do so, we will always have the competition beating us. One's ability to compete in markets is also the ability to think differently and to convert the current situation's disadvantages in our favour.

16

THE NEXT GENERATION: INVOLVE THEM YOUNG

Mukesh Ambani's wife and children have also been getting involved in the business. They are playing important roles within Reliance's various verticals.

His daughter, Isha, graduated from the Stanford Graduate School of Business (an MBA, 2018) and Yale University (in Psychology and South Asian studies, 2014). She has also worked with McKinsey & Company as a consultant. She joined the boards of Reliance Retail and Reliance Jio in October 2014. She headed the Reliance's e-commerce initiative into

Persevere and Prevail Like Mukesh Ambani

fashion retail in 2016, by launching Ajio, an online shopping portal. She is married to Anand Piramal, son of billionaire Ajay Piramal, whose interests range from pharmaceuticals to real estate.[148]

At an interview given during her wedding, Isha recalled her years growing up in the Ambani household. She said that her mother wanted to be a full-time mother, but she went back to work when they were just five, yet remained a tiger mom. Isha also stated that her parents ensured that all of them learnt the value of money, hard work and humility, despite their privileged background. She also stated that she had seen her father work very hard in chasing his dream to take Reliance to the great levels that it is today. Isha also appreciated the fact that in spite of Mukesh working long hours, he was always there whenever his children needed him.[149]

---

[148] P.R. Sanjai, Bloomberg, 'Asia's Richest Man Grooms the Heirs to His $50 Billion Fortune', MSN.com, accessed 16 August 2019, https://www.msn.com/en-in/money/news/asias-richest-man-grooms-the-heirs-to-his-dollar50-billion-fortune/ar-AAFRDP1?li=AAgfW3S#page=2; *The Times of India*, accessed 23 September 2019, https://timesofindia.indiatimes.com/topic/isha-ambani

[149] 'Mukesh and Nita Ambani had kids Isha and Akash via IVF after 7 years of marriage', *India Today*, 31 January 2019, accessed September 2019, https://www.indiatoday.in/lifestyle/celebrity/

Isha's twin brother, Akash, is an alumnus of Brown University (in Economics). He married his childhood sweetheart, Shloka Mehta, the daughter of a Mumbai-based diamond trader and jeweller, Russell Mehta, CEO-owner of Rosy Blue Diamonds.[150] He is currently the chief of strategy in Reliance Jio.

Anant, their younger brother, is expected to also take key responsibilities in the future.

As mentioned earlier, the twin siblings, Isha and Akash, have been appointed to the board of Jio and Reliance Retail Ventures Ltd in 2014.[151]

Mukesh has attributed the credit for his entering the Internet business to his children. Mukesh went on to say,

> My son Akash said, 'Dad, your generation doesn't get it. In the old world, telecom was a voice—and you only made money when one person calls and

---

story/mukesh-and-nita-ambani-had-kids-isha-and-akash-via-ivf-after-7-years-of-marriage-1443614-2019-01-31

[150] P.R. Sanjai, *Bloomberg*, 'Asia's Richest Man Grooms the Heirs to His $50 Billion Fortune', MSN.com, accessed 16 August 2019, https://www.msn.com/en-in/money/news/asias-richest-man-grooms-the-heirs-to-his-dollar50-billion-fortune/ar-AAFRDP1?li=AAgfW3S#page=2; *The Times of India*, accessed 23 September 2019, https://timesofindia.indiatimes.com/topic/akash-ambani

[151] Ibid.

the other answers. In our new world, everything is digital. We can do a lot more with a digital network than just talk'. Isha and Akash belong to India's young generation that is far more creative, far more ambitious and far more impatient to become the best in the world. These young Indians convinced me that broadband Internet is the defining technology of our age and India cannot be left behind.[152]

These words appear prophetic, as it did lead Mukesh to invest around $35 billion into Jio[153], to enter the mobile phone market and be amongst the top four players by offering free voice call services and high data speeds at very low prices. This then paved the path for Jio fibre which connected homes and offices with fibre-optic cables, to deliver content and Internet, again at high speeds and low costs.

Since that time, they have been appearing at annual shareholder meetings and addressing investors, and

---

[152]PTI, 'Jio was first seeded by Isha Ambani in 2011, reveals dad Mukesh', *The Economic Times*, 16 March 2018

[153]Newley Purnell, 'Two Years Ago, India Lacked Fast, Cheap Internet—One Billionaire Changed All That', *The Wall Street Journal*, 5 September 2018, accessed 15 August 2019, https://www.wsj.com/articles/two-years-ago-india-lacked-fast-cheap-Internetone-billionaire-changed-all-that-1536159916?mod=e2tw

introducing new products. At the 42nd Reliance AGM, on 12 August 2019, they took the stage to demonstrate a range of applications such as virtual reality and conference calls, which would be an additional service with Reliance Jio fibre, a new high-speed data network that RIL was planning to commercially launch on 5 September later that year. The future seems to be bright for Jio, given that the next generation is spearheading their initiatives in the digital space, and these are also the biggest consumers of digital content. These are the 'digital natives', the generation which has grown up in the era of constant digital inputs environment. So they will be the best guides to direct the future direction of the company.

NITA AMBANI

Any story on Mukesh Ambani would be incomplete without a chapter on his wife, Nita. If Mukesh is the story of commercial success and Reliance, then Nita is the driving force behind the success of the non-commercial part of Reliance. She has been an active proponent, driving initiatives in education, health, sports and revival of the arts, and well-deserving of her title as the first lady of Indian business. She has played a very important role which may not have got

Persevere and Prevail Like Mukesh Ambani

its true recognition in the media.

She is involved in academics and has started 14 schools at the various locations where Mukesh has set up plants.[154]

In 2017, she had been a recipient of the Rashtriya Khel Protsahan Puraskar on behalf of the Reliance Foundation, from the President of India. She started the 'Education for all' programme with the Mumbai Indians (a franchise cricket team based in the city of Mumbai), which reached out to 100,000 underprivileged children. She also set up the Reliance Foundation Jr. NBA programme for encouraging basketball at the grass-roots level. This was soon followed by other projects such as the Reliance Foundation Young Champs (which has 45 per cent female participants!) and the Reliance Foundation Youth Sports (RFYS).

She recalled the time when she was at a global conference with her husband in 2014 when the FIFA World Cup was being played. She avidly remembered feeling left out at the time, since there was no national team that they could cheer for, like all the other participants in the conference. This led to their desire

---

[154]Tanya Chaitanya, 'Nita Mukesh Ambani: The power of purpose', *Femina*, 24 October 2017, accessed 23 September 2019, https://www.femina.in/celebs/indian/nita-mukesh-ambani-the-power-of-purpose-66223.html

to set up a soccer league, thus reviving the Indian Super League, which had been started by Reliance and the late Ted Forstmann (of IMG). RFYS started with football in 2016 and added athletics in 2017. The programme had an impact, with the foundation reaching out to over seven million children across its various initiatives along with increasing the female participation by 170 per cent by 2017.

Nita believes that sports and education should be used to empower girls, and we should make every effort as a nation to achieve this. And these efforts should come at the grass-roots level. These achievements may have played a role when she was elected as the first Indian woman member of the International Olympics Committee in 2016 during the Rio Olympics, in which, incidentally, three Indian women—Sakshi Malik, P.V. Sindhu and Dipa Karmakar—had won medals.

She has also involved Reliance Foundation in rebuilding schools in Uttarakhand with two schools built, complete with playgrounds, infrastructure and toilets, after it had been affected by floods.

Nita also worked to reach out to women in villages and make them self-reliant. Vajaben, a single mother from a marginalized community, was able to grow enough to provide for her own family, and to sell to others with the help of the Reliance Foundation. This lady encouraged others to do the same and became the president of that village farmers' association.[155]

Nita also took over the management of the Mumbai Indians, their IPL team which she handed over to her elder son Akash to manage.[156]

Sir H.N. Reliance Foundation Hospital and Research Centre is another of her projects. This was opened in 2014, to provide affordable, human-touch oriented, international-quality healthcare. The hospital is credited with numerous path-breaking surgeries and medical procedures which have saved many lives. It conducted Mumbai's first robot-assisted kidney transplant, which reduces the incisions, thus speeding up patients' recoveries.[157]

She raised her children while handling her academic projects, and used to pick up her children from school and take them to her office where they finished their homework. Nita was then also appointed as the first woman director on the Board of Reliance Industries.[158]

Her journey has been one of learning from her children. Even though they have now joined the businesses, she has learnt her technological skills

---

[155] Ibid.
[156] Ibid.
[157] Ibid.
[158] Ibid.

from them. Additionally, she appreciates the new-age people management skills working as friends, in open offices, which are present in Jio. That everybody could sit together and interact openly brought in equality, ideas and freshness. Besides, this also made work fun for her.[159]

A passionate believer in gender equality, Nita believes that one should educate boys and girls equally from their childhood and there should be no difference between them. She also feels that one should let girls decide their life path and encourage them to make their own choices.[160]

She relates the example of her daughter Isha, whom she encouraged to dream and follow them. She encouraged her daughter to reach for the stars. She stated that her aspiration for her children is for them to be happy, find their path and for them to know that they will always have their parents' backing and support. She stated that her children had found their interests. The youngest son, Anant, was compassionate towards animals and wanted to work for the environment, close to Mother Nature. Her eldest son, Akash, had an interest in technology and was involved in Jio and

---

[159]Ibid.
[160]Ibid.

Isha was initially working in Jio but had moved on to her dream of learning.[161]

Nita is dedicated to her family. She considers Mukesh to be quiet and reflective, whereas she sees herself as an extrovert who likes to meet people. She does not like to watch movies like her husband. She remarked that she was fortunate that Mukesh had unconditional love for the family, and he made the time to be at home spending time with the children if Nita was busy with the school and Jamnagar projects.[162]

Both Nita and Mukesh make the effort to spend time with their children. They go on holidays together, usually twice a year to Africa. Their visits are so frequent that the children joke that they have not seen the rest of the world, as they were always in Africa and that even the lions recognize them there. But the fact that they are away from the world, alone amidst nature's grandeur, is what excites them.[163]

In 2019, Mukesh and Nita Ambani celebrated their son Akash's wedding with Shloka Mehta, with the members of the Army, Navy, Mumbai Police, paramilitary forces and the Railway Protection force

---

[161] Ibid.
[162] Ibid.
[163] Ibid.

and their families. This was a celebration which was over and above any other event that they had organized for the wedding.[164] This was their way of expressing gratitude and solidarity with the people who contributed to making the nation and the city safer, besides seeking their blessings for their son's wedding.

On the occasion, she reiterated Reliance Foundation's commitment 'to take full responsibility of the education, employment, and livelihood needs of the families of our martyrs.'[165] She announced that Reliance Foundation was establishing a skill-development centre exclusively for the armed forces and their families. 'We as a family very much identify with the city's socio-cultural fabric and have deep respect and gratitude for the people who make it function, particularly our police, armed forces, and city workers. It is at once humbling and immensely satisfying for us that we can share our joy with this

---

[164]ANI, 'Nita, Mukesh Ambani celebrate son's wedding with men in uniform, their families', Aninews, 12 March 2019, accessed 23 September 2019, https://www.aninews.in/news/entertainment/out-of-box/nita-mukesh-ambani-celebrate-sons-wedding-with-men-in-uniform-their-families20190312222803/

[165]PTI New Delhi, 'Reliance Foundation offers to take responsibility of families of martyred CRPF jawans', *The Hindu BusinessLine*, 16 February 2019

great city to which we owe everything', she said.[166]

Indeed, Nita remains a purpose-driven wife, mother and philanthropist! In spite of the plenty that surrounds the family, she has worked on giving back to society, in areas where the society's needs are the most, e.g. education, healthcare, care for the girl child and upliftment of the economically deprived by giving them livelihoods. This is the other side of Reliance which is away from the media, but in no ways any less significant!

---

[166] ANI, 'Nita, Mukesh Ambani celebrate son's wedding with men in uniform, their families', Aninews, 12 March 2019, accessed 23 September 2019, https://www.aninews.in/news/entertainment/out-of-box/nita-mukesh-ambani-celebrate-sons-wedding-with-men-in-uniform-their-families20190312222803/

17
VALUES

At heart, I was born middle-class. It stayed in our Gujarati middle-class parents, and those really have never gone out of us. I think that is a good thing. For all of us, the small pleasures of life don't go away. I am very, very proud of the values that I have inherited.

—Mukesh Ambani[167]

---

[167]Manu Balachandran, 'India's richest man still thinks he is "middle-class" at heart', *Quartz India*, 18 October 2016, , accessed 10 September 2019, https://qz.com/india/811959/mukesh-ambani-indias-richest-man-still-thinks-he-is-middle-class-at-heart/

Value is a controversial point which leads to agitated discussions whenever it is raised. But the Ambanis are known to strictly follow certain non-negotiable values.

VEGETARIANISM

There was a time when Reliance Retail was selling frozen non-vegetarian foods under the brand name 'Delight'.

There were objections raised by certain sections of the community, particularly the consumers, shareholders and investors, whose religious sentiments were hurt. The non-vegetarian foods business was a profitable one, growing at a Compound Annual Growth Rate (CAGR) of 25 to 30 per cent, and was estimated to be about 10 per cent of the company's total retail business. Reliance sources felt that certain sections of customers were reluctant to shop at Reliance stores.

Here is a history of the non-vegetarian foods business to add to the context for better understanding. Reliance had invested in a 45 per cent stake of Two Sisters Foods India, which was owned by 2 Sisters Food Group (2SFG). 2SFG was the third-largest food company in the United Kingdom and was a supplier to the retail, food-service and food manufacturing

Values

sectors supplying poultry, red meat, fish and chilled/frozen products.

Reliance had invested about ₹50 crore in Delight stores. It had established a presence with more than 100 stores across 25 cities in 11 states. An exclusive, completely different supply chain was made for Delight, catering to the preferences and philosophies of various customers. The plan was to scale-up Delight to eventually have 1,000 stores since non-vegetarian products have a margin of 20 to 25 per cent as compared to the 10 to 15 per cent margins in food and grocery retailing.

As a result of this request to reconsider the non-vegetarian food product sales, Reliance decided to completely exit from the non-vegetarian food business. It cancelled its joint-venture and wrote off the investment in Delight. This was done keeping in mind the sentiments of the customers, and for Reliance to be more relevant to a broader segment of customers and to enable them to leverage their core competencies.

It was also noted that since Mukesh himself is a strict vegetarian, it was a clear signal that business decisions remain inseparable from an individual's dietary and lifestyle choices.[168] An observer stated that

---

[168]Piyush Pandey, 'No delight for RIL's non-veg buyers', *The Times*

fear dominates greed in many cases, and 'Tradition, culture and ethos of Mukesh Ambani prevailed over economic, finance and commercial considerations.'[169]

LEARNINGS

The shutting down of the non-vegetarian foods business by Reliance Retail showed that values were non-negotiable.

Incidentally, I have visited Harikishandas Hospital in Mumbai, run by Reliance Foundation, which is also a vegetarian hospital!

Managers have to understand that businesses will reflect the values of the family owning the business and these cannot conflict. The faster managers understand this, the easier is the integration into the businesses. Similarly, this could be an advantage for family businesses, over professionally run businesses, as the value system of the family will permeate everything that the business does. This serves as a powerful tool for differentiating family businesses.

Yes, there are other viewpoints, such as, these

---

of India, 16 December 2013, accessed 26 September 2019, https://timesofindia.indiatimes.com/business/india-business/No-delight-for-RILs-non-veg-buyers/articleshow/27443212.cms
[169]Ibid.

Values

could also prove to be obstacles impeding the growth of family-owned firms, but one cannot argue against any business having values which they hold dear. These values like integrity, treating people fairly, etc. are timeless and cut across geographies and industries. Increasingly, we are seeing businesses adopt these values and hold everyone responsible for adhering to these. This is only a precursor for the things to come.

18

A LOW-COST MODEL FOR INDIAN MARKETS: IF IT DOES NOT EXIST, BUILD ONE!

JIO NETWORK AND LOW COSTS

Mukesh Ambani had been inspired by the lowest-cost form of communication, the humble postcard costing 40 paise, to set the price of a call, when he had first launched the Monsoon Hungama offer, in July 2003 in the days of Reliance Infocomm.

This was the precursor to his next step, to bring 4G smartphone prices to affordable levels. Mukesh

A Low-cost Model for Indian Markets

knew that over 50 per cent of all the world devices were made in China, so he started spending more time there. His visits were followed up by Jio personnel, seeking to introduce a low-cost phone as the then-available brands were too expensive for Jio's plans to address the needs of millions of customers. It was to address this need, that the LYF phone was created. This was a global effort with designers from various countries such as China, Germany, England, Israel and the US working on this. They worked on developing a new phone from scratch and after a year's effort, were able to develop the LYF phone at a price of ₹4,000, a price point which was 25 per cent of the then-prevailing prices.[170]

The LYF phones captured 7 per cent market share within months of its launch, in the first quarter of 2016. These phones were also sold out due to the high demand in some locations. The low prices soon caused other low-cost phones to come into the market. As a result, the 4G smartphone user base shot up from 86 million to 178 million between September 2016 and September 2017 with the Jio user base also increasing

---

[170]'Mukesh Ambani's army of expats at Jio', *LiveMint*, accessed 23 September 2019, https://www.livemint.com/Industry/lHFD4WXCoWs4BPdiYgdFKJ/Mukesh-Ambanis-army-of-expats-at-Jio.html

from 16 million to 139 million.

This pursuit, for making affordable products, lead to the Jio Phone, which further reduced the prices to the levels of a feature-phone. Jio then realized that the ₹4,000 price tag was too high for new phones and it had to find some other way. So the design team came up with the Jio Phone at an even lower price! They worked on the lowest possible experience that the users would need and they designed the phone keeping this in mind. This helped bring the prices down to feature-phone levels. This move also led to a lot of competitors in the form of network operators bundling low-cost smartphones from companies such as Micromax, Karbonn, Intex and Lava with services that caused the data industry to be severely disrupted.[171]

LEARNINGS

The above shows that Mukesh Ambani has gone deep into understanding his customer. He understands the needs and the price points on which they will be able to buy and he delivers a product catering to those needs. He did not take what was offered if it was not

---

[171] Ibid.

acceptable to his audience. On the contrary, he moved to invent products which fit his purpose, which gave him an advantage over his rivals. The fact that he is operating on perhaps the largest volumes ever in the world, does make his job a lot easier!

Oftentimes entrepreneurs or managers get stuck when faced with adversity or trying situations. At this time, most of us, usually accept what is given to us, as non-changeable and fixed. What we can learn from here is to consider whether we can work around the biggest constraint and try to gain an advantage.

SUMMARY

Let us summarize what we have learnt till now.

Mukesh Ambani as a person is hard-working, humble and sets a personal example. Leaders need to be a model for their people and set an example for others to follow and serve as an inspiration. He leads a simple lifestyle with simple tastes, shunning brands.

His management style is focussed on global markets with large-scale capacities to serve these markets. He benchmarks with global leaders and experts to get the best access to technologies and experience. He is in favour of setting up professional processes and systems. He wants to attract and retain young talent who are professionally qualified, competent and experienced. He believes in empowering them to learn new things. He is also willing to listen to the next generation to understand where the world is headed and is willing to learn from them. His focus on detail for any project and voracious desire to learn serves him well. In his childhood, he has witnessed first-hand a life of hardship and has learnt life-lessons from his father, his teacher and in school.

He has learnt the 'value of including time' in the cost equation. He works on the basis that saving time is more important than saving capital and hence for his capital projects, he is willing to spend more money if it gives him a time advantage. This has been the secret of his ability to commission all his projects before time. Another case in point being his installation of all the piping in his refinery before the plant was shipped and then fitting the plant within the pipelines.

Integration and flexibility of the value chain: Mukesh has followed the strategy which his father, Dhirubhai, had perfected, of integrating backwards into the value chain. This way, he is able to derive benefits from integration besides having greater control over his processes. Mukesh has kept the ability to cater to different markets with different products to get higher profitability. He has also built flexibility in his plants, which give him greater control over the types of raw materials he can use and the finished goods that he can produce. Earlier, he had worked with export markets when the domestic markets were not as profitable or large. Then he moved to different product-mixes to get higher profits. His Jamnagar refinery can handle a range of inputs including the cheaper types which no one usually buys. This is the cornerstone of his strategy in operations.

Look for future opportunities: Mukesh has been looking for opportunities for the future. He has been constantly on the lookout for areas of growth. He has been investing in the petrochemicals and oil sector to keep the current cash flow ongoing. He has also invested in retail and mobile network space.

The power of teams: Mukesh understands the importance of teams and having competent, qualified people operating with him. He also hires people from all over the world.

Reduce debt: Mukesh realizes that the new environment needs him to reduce debt and he has accordingly worked on doing that in his company. He has strategic investors who have invested in his company and he has used these funds to repay his loans. He has been proactive in trying to become debt-free in the next two to three years.

Global-scale capacities. Think big: Mukesh has always considered competing on a global scale. He has not been restricted by domestic markets. This principle has guided his investments in plant capacities and markets. In fact, he has surpassed most of his competitors globally and his capacities are amongst the top three in the world. This has given him huge operational advantages in terms of costs and efficiencies.

Diversify into areas for higher growth: Mukesh has grown into the retail and mobile space in pursuit of higher growth rates. Leaders have to learn how to operate in competitive markets.

The interesting learning here is that Mukesh was not the first entrant into this space (whether digital or mobile). He came in later and used the late entry to his advantage by not making the mistakes that the earlier players had made. He also learnt that selling basic products will not make sense and one will have to find ways to offer innovative products by which he can raise his margins. This is a new space, where most products are given away free, there is very little government control or regulation, there is a lot of competition (usually from global players) and the customer can choose to walk away to any other competitor very easily. Hence, it requires a different approach to play this game, that of higher value addition. He is doing this in the petrochemical space (by investing in higher value-added chemicals), in the mobile space (by moving into value-added services of movies—first day-first show, music) and in retail (by tie-ups with foreign brands for stores in India and working out the online retail model).

Look for higher value addition opportunities and create new opportunities: Reliance has been growing by looking at how it can cater to higher-margin areas and moving away from focussing on the commodity markets. It is following this strategy in the petrol, chemical and oil business, retail and in the mobile verticals. Also, it is hunting for newer ways to make money from existing opportunities.

The voice of the next generation: Listen to the next generation to figure out what they are talking about, to understand what the environment is and what their requirements are. Mukesh has the patience and the willingness to listen to new-age consumers and understand them.

Values: Businesses reflect the values of the family

behind the business. This plays an important role in defining the businesses, what they will do and what they won't do.

Low-cost models for the Indian markets: Mukesh has been designing models based on what the Indian markets need, and custom designing products and services relevant to the Indian markets. This has helped them understand and compete better in the Indian markets.

END NOTE

Mukesh Ambani has come a long way, with his father having navigated from Aden in Yemen to Bhuleshwar, from Usha Kiran at Altamount Road to Sea Wind, to eventually Mukesh arriving at Antilia.[172]

When I was researching to write this book, I was often asked 'What is the secret of his success?' Or 'What drives Mukesh Ambani to become the richest man in the country and still keep on going?'

---

[172]Sucheta Dalal and Debashis Basu, 'The arbitrage in farm produce is much bigger than that in software services—Mukesh Ambani', Moneylife.in, 13 April 2010, accessed 15 August 2019, https://www.moneylife.in/article/the-arbitrage-in-farm-produce-is-much-bigger-than-that-in-software-services-mukesh-ambani/4744.html

Persevere and Prevail Like Mukesh Ambani

The spectacular success of Mukesh Ambani, which has been repeated in every industry that he has entered, has shown that he has a formula, if you will, which he uses to replicate his success. What I have tried to do here, is to derive some understanding of what he has done, and then work backwards in trying to explain and understand his moves.

There have been some press reports on the ability of the Ambanis to ensure a favourable regulatory and political environment for themselves. But as we have seen in recent instances of the business scenario (that is, in September 2019) with the National Company Law Tribunal (NCLT) auctions and various cases of business houses being in trouble, that may not be true. We see that there were many business houses that were following, what some in the press have labelled as 'crony capitalism'. Some believe that this is a legacy of doing business in India. (On a different note, there are some very reputable business houses too, who have been untarnished and still preserve their spotless reputations.) Mukesh has stated in an earlier chapter that all such claims are 'fables'.

But what remains to be understood is that Mukesh, or for that matter, any other industrialist or business house, would perhaps have not been successful, unless they were able to make a product which was affordable

Summary

and cost-effective.

Now I think that leaders should probably take a larger viewpoint and not get fixated on this. If we look at business history, we see that a lot of companies and business houses who gained licences during the licence raj did not make it once liberalization was ushered into India. Now, they may have got a headstart and may have also made obscene profits. But the companies that did not innovate or stay current with the customer needs usually perished.

Therefore, what leaders need to see, in the case of Mukesh, is the ability to dream big and execute fast. He has also got to the bottom of any industry that he enters into and works out ways to make his companies more profitable, usually by reinventing what others may have taken for granted. For him, nothing is a constraint or cannot be redesigned. He has a very good understanding and knowledge of the environment he operates in, perhaps better than anyone else. He is a voracious reader, works hard and challenges some of the best brains globally, using bleeding-edge technologies to simplify the complex and to repackage it in a way that makes it profitable. And that is the lesson that leaders should emulate.

Any advantage is temporary. But Mukesh has understood this and hence is constantly working on the next two or three mountains to climb, while his competitors are still battling his last salvo. He is looking at the future, not as an eventuality, but as an environment where his scale and vision can influence it and shape it, hopefully in his favour.

The magnitude of his visions and ambitions, when he does talk about them, are scary to some, and most people scoff at them. But the admirable part is that he has executed flawlessly and achieved what he said he would. And that is something that most competitors have come to realize, if at all, rather belatedly, that you do not underestimate Mukesh's ability to execute what he dreams.

Having changed two industries (textile and petrochemicals), he is now getting ready to roll out his magic in two other industries (retail and telecom) where some of his competitors are bleeding. Mukesh has radically changed every industry he has entered—even if he is not the first entrant but a late entrant. There is no doubt, that his plans for Jio and Reliance Retail will be heavily influenced by his vision, which has always been on a very large scale. The only difference this time is that these are arenas where now his competitors are larger global players who are preparing to enter India. Mukesh is just getting started, preparing his company by investing heavily in both these sectors.

Summary

This is a story that is going to be worth watching as it unfolds. We have front row seats, and it is just beginning.